E-MOTIONS

How to Work With the Head and the Hand Without Losing the Heart

Mastering Emotional Intelligence: The Gateway to Deeper Connections, Mental Well-being and Productivity

Abraham O. Owoseni, Ph.D.

E-Motions : How to Work with the Head and the Hand Without
Losing the Heart
Copyright © 2023 Abraham O. Owoseni
Published by MindMould

Scripture quotations are from the Holy Bible and their respective
versions.

For further information, permission, book orders, training and
speaking engagements, please contact:

Website: www.abrahamowoseni.com

E-mails: books@abrahamowoseni.com

              training@abrahamowoseni.com

Cover Design by Kenneth Ezugwu
Editorial by Kelechi Benita-Maria Opara
Book Formatting by Derek Murphy

First Edition: November 2023

Welcome to "E-motions: How to Lead With the Head and the Hand Without Losing the Heart." As you begin this journey, I invite you to append your name and today's date to mark the beginning of your experience with this book. Also, please reflect on your goals and expectations for this reading adventure and make a note of it below.

Name

____

Date

____

Your Expectations and Goals

____

____

____

____

____

____

Thank you for taking the first step. Enjoy the adventure!

"E-Motions" is a profound and timely guide that addresses the critical issue of balancing emotional intelligence with professional efficiency. In an age where technology often overshadows our human essence, Owoseni's methodology shines as a beacon of wisdom. His 'immutable' truth, "Your emotions are ever in motion, but you are the driver behind the steering wheel," resonates deeply. This book empowers you to harmonise your mind and actions while preserving the core of your humanity. It's a transformative journey towards emotional mastery, mental well-being, and genuine connections—a must-read for those seeking a fulfilling life filled with peace, resilience, healing, and happiness. Embrace this book for your personal and professional growth.

Johnson Abbaly
Founder,
The Smartan House

Activating Wonderful Experiences So One May Enjoy, or A.W.E.S.O.M.E, isn't just an acronym; it's my name and my nature. I firmly believe that this sense of wonder and joy can become as natural as breathing for every individual on this planet through the harmony of heart and brain. It's a journey that Dr. Abraham Owoseni's book, "E-motion: How to Work With the Head and the Hand Without Losing the Heart " seeks to unlock, revealing the key to unlocking the incredible potential within us all.

Dr Joshua Awesome
Founder/ Coaching Psychologist, African Institute of Mind
South Africa

As a psychologist, I have been exposed to uncountable books on emotions for over two decades. None of the books both nationally and internationally is as practical, straightforward, and hands-on as this masterpiece by Dr. Abraham Owoseni. In my role as a Clinical Psychologist and Psychotherapist, I have seen the disintegration of marriages, relationships, family bonds, and even workplace convivial relationships that could have been saved if the parties involved had displayed just an iota of emotional intelligence. In this book, leaders, professionals, young and older people will easily understand that although their emotions are always in motion, they are the drivers of their emotions and can decide to drive their emotions to a pleasant destination. This book will teach you how to pay attention to where you are driving. If you want to build lifelong connections, nurture relationships, and establish professional networks amongst others, I strongly and unreservedly recommend "E-motions: How to Work with the Head and the Hand without Losing the Heart" by Dr. Abraham Owoseni because it is a life-transforming book.

David O. Igbokwe, PhD
Head, Department of Psychology, Baze University Abuja,
Visiting Senior Lecturer, Nile University of Nigeria
Former Stress Counsellor, World Health Organisation (WHO),
Nigeria Country Office, Abuja, FCT, Nigeria

This book isn't just a must-read; it's a game-changer. Dr. Owoseni skillfully blends practical wisdom with profound insights for navigating the intricacies of emotions in "E-motions," employing the analogy of driving a car on the highway. In this masterpiece, he unveils the tools for harnessing emotional intelligence to turbocharge connections, bolster mental well-being, and skyrocket productivity. Whether aspiring for professional success, yearning for extraordinary personal growth, or seeking life-giving relationships, "E-motions" unlocks irrefutable transformation and transcendence. Read, study, and share this treasure!

Oluchi Ihekuna, CEO Avant Garde Health Services

The Book— "E-Motions" brilliantly captures the essence of the heart, head, and hand synergy in the pursuit of a purposeful existence, strengthening meaningful connections, and ultimately attaining happiness through a life of impact. Dr. Owoseni employs vivid automotive analogies, touching on themes like highways, licenses, traffic, roadblocks, brakes, and lubrication, to drive home the need for developing emotional mastery. The wisdom within this book is deserving of integration into the curricula of our primary and secondary educational institutions, to engender national development over the coming decades.

Toni Nathaniel, KidsInspiring Nation

I love that the writer used relatable examples to explain emotional intelligence. In a world where people focus mostly on the external, this book calls you back to the inside world which is the realer world. This book will help you shift your focus to the world within and help you pay more attention to your spirit. I particularly love how the writer emphasized that God gave us emotions but we tend to shut out our emotions and brace up. Meanwhile, we ought to leverage our emotions to brace up. If you find yourself dwindling in your emotions and struggling to regulate your inner world and balance, this book is what you need.

Enifome Ogbimi,
Executive Director, Live Again Foundation
Author, How to Become a New You.

The lessons drawn from the book are intended to help a wide spectrum of audience particularly with managing their emotions. Every read is a scintillating experience, it is my absolute pleasure to recommend this book for all; it is such an impactful and interesting read.

Kingsley Okere, MBA, MSc, MCIPM
MD, Kemslis Pragmatic Ltd

The book proffers practical strategies that can help you clear emotional roadblocks, maintain a steady and harmonious emotional flow, build resilience to overcome life's challenges and have a deep understanding of the diverse emotions of others. Highly recommended for everyone in all walks of life; it is useful for everyone who desires an improvement in their relationships with others as well as those who desire to effectively trade the relationship currency.

Olubunmi Izebere
Life Coach/Relationship Manager
Author, Preserved for His Purpose

Dr Owoseni's work highlights the stark reality that the growing digital landscape may threaten genuine human connections, in both private and professional relationships. This book is a much-needed reminder that our close relationships are not a luxury but a biological necessity for our mental and physical well-being.

Dr. Abbie Maroño, Author of "Work in Progress"
Behavioral Scientist and Director of Education
Orlando, Florida

Through clear and relatable storytelling, Abraham underscores the vital role of human connections and relationships in achieving personal, professional, and business success. His remarkable writing culminates in a compelling call to embrace a transcendent life, inviting readers to seek the guiding influence of God's Spirit in the mastery of our emotions. Whether you are a business or corporate leader, an early or mid-career professional, this book serves as an invaluable companion on your leadership journey.

Abimbola O Adebakin
Founder/CEO, Advantage Health Africa
Lagos, Nigeria

In this masterpiece, from the stable of the prolific author, Dr. Abraham Owoseni, avid readers are exposed to the what, why, and how of emotional intelligence in attaining personal growth and professional success. The author provided invaluable and practical insights to mastering the fundamental principles essential in building a high emotional quotient. An investment of quality time in divulging the content of this insightful and inspiring book will empower the reader to master the delicate art of working in harmony with intellect, skill, and emotion which are highly essential to making exploits and lasting impact on the earth. I strongly recommend - "E-Motions: How to Work with the Head and the Hand without Losing the Heart" as a must-read to every individual, professional, leader and executive to reignite the profound significance of emotional intelligence in our homes, work places, faith-based communities and the nation at large.

Kola Oyelade
CEO, Candlelit Educational Consult

Embark on a transformative journey through the pages of "E-Motions- How to Work with the Head and Hand without Losing the Heart." This book takes you on a journey towards the intricate terrain of self-discovery, exploring the motivations behind our actions and offering a roadmap for emotional mastery. This insightful trip invites readers to buckle up for a fulfilling and intentional existence, navigating the ever-changing landscapes of life with self-awareness and purpose.
I loved the energy felt in this book.

Faten El Ayache
Executive Coach and Trainer
Dubai

I am delighted to express my commendation for Dr. Abraham Owoseni and the remarkable work he has accomplished with his latest title. Since 2014, Dr. Owoseni has been a source of blessing to thousands through his impactful workshops, books, seminars, and more. Personally, encountering his work has been profoundly enriching. The subtitle of this book, "How to Work With the Head and the Hand Without Losing your Heart," resonates deeply with me. In our fast-paced world, it's evident that some individuals, while intellectually sharp, may appear heartless. Unfortunately, many are not equipped with the essential skills for self-regulation, empathy, and fostering meaningful connections. As a result, countless individuals enter adulthood feeling lost and disconnected, setting the stage for a chaotic life. This is why "E-Motions" is exceptionally timely. The book is a treasure trove of rich, straightforward content, presented in an easy-to-read manner with practical and actionable ideas. It is a valuable resource for everyone. "E-Motions" is a book that transcends boundaries; its wisdom is accessible and applicable to readers of all backgrounds.

Ade Owolabi
The Marriage Evangelist

"E-motions" is more than a book; it is an odyssey into the depths of human emotion and the spiritual essence that underpins our existence. Dr. Owoseni's writing is not just informative; it is transformative, igniting a spark of enthusiasm in readers to embrace their emotions, understand them, and ultimately harness their power for a more balanced and fulfilling life.

Dr. Niyi Borire
Director of Southwest Neurology
Lecturer, University of New South Wales, Australia

I see him as a master life designer; he has influenced thousands of lives the world over through his speaking engagements, books, and most importantly, his life.
David Igbokwe, PhD

I can best describe him as someone who impacts lives with the entirety of his being.
Omotola Olori

He is someone who obviously knows his onions and is confident in what the "Manufacturer" has called him to do – and the fruits are obvious!
Tola Adefidipe, Canada

Abraham is one of the most passionate speakers I have ever met; his passion for youth empowerment is exceptional. He is the pure example of the kind of leaders and change-makers the world needs.
Daniel Ojinaka

His inspiring words can never go stale. He continues to release truth and words of wisdom for the current and future generations.
Damilola Eluyela, Australia

He has his own unique way of teaching that will never leave you the same.
Emmanuel Adeifa

One of the most eloquent and passionate speakers and mentors I ever met.
Sonia Jerry-Okondu

Contents

Dedication

Foreword

This book is a guide crafted for anyone navigating the complexities of modern life. Whether you find yourself grappling with workplace disengagement, strained personal relationships, or the pervasive challenges of stress and burnout, here is your compass to rediscover the essence of humanity. Designed for seasoned leaders, aspiring professionals, and individuals seeking emotional well-being, it provides practical tools and insights to master the delicate art of harmonizing intellect, skill, and emotion.

Join this expedition for healing, rejuvenation, and the wisdom to create a life rich in meaningful connections. It's your roadmap to not only professional success but also profound personal growth. If you have picked up this book to read through, then it is only right that I Welcome you to an extraordinary exploration of the human experience, where emotions are not mere fleeting sensations, but the fuel that propels us through the intricate highways of life.

In "E-motions: How to Work with the Head and Hand without Losing the Heart," Dr. Abraham O. Owoseni extends an invitation to a transformative journey that transcends conventional self-help literature, seamlessly weaving together psychology, spirituality, and real-life anecdotes. From the opening pages, Dr. Owoseni captivates readers with a compelling narrative, drawing us into a world where emotions are the drivers of our existence. The author skillfully intertwines Newton's laws of motion with the fluidity of emotions, providing readers with a unique perspective on their emotional states. The narrative evolves into an introspective journey, prompting readers to ask why they drive the way they do.

The chapters of this book unfold as beacons of self-discovery, navigating through the realms of self-awareness, self-regulation, and motivation. Dr. Owoseni doesn't just offer insights; he empowers readers with practical tools to navigate their emotional landscapes, transforming setbacks into stepping-stones toward personal growth. Empathy and social skills become the pillars of interpersonal relationships, drawing parallels between the maintenance of emotional well-being and the care and servicing of vehicles. The metaphorical "OIL" of human relations—Offer value, Invest in relationships, Look away from selfish interests—becomes a guiding principle for building meaningful connections in the navigation of human interaction.

Dr. Owoseni skillfully illuminates the spiritual core as the foundation of our being, offering a profound perspective on the attacks the soul faces in the modern world. A call to surrender to a higher power resonates as a beacon of hope, reminding readers that they are not alone on their journey. "E-motions" is more than a book; it is an odyssey into the depths of human emotion and the spiritual essence that underpins our existence. Dr. Owoseni's writing is not just informative; it is transformative, igniting a spark of enthusiasm in readers to embrace their emotions, understand them, and ultimately harness their power for a more balanced and fulfilling life.

Prepare to be captivated, inspired, and guided through a journey that goes beyond intellect, touching the heart, and resonating with the spirit. "E-motions" is a testament to Dr. Owoseni's commitment to guiding individuals toward a holistic and balanced life—a life where emotions are not just experienced but embraced, understood, and ultimately transformed for the better.

Get ready for an expedition into the heart of what it means to be human—a journey that promises to leave you enlightened, empowered, and eager to navigate life's highways with newfound emotional intelligence. I thoroughly enjoyed my experience on this transformative journey.

Dr. Niyi Borire

Award-winning Neurologist, Neuroscientist,
NeuroLeadership Expert, Lecturer, Speaker and Change Agent
Convener, Legacy Conference

Sydney, Australia
November 2023

Introduction

IN THE MIDST OF OUR FAST-PACED DAILY ROUTINES and the ever-advancing tide of technology, it often appears that we have fewer opportunities for genuine human connections. The very essence of our humanity seems to face increasing challenges. Whether you're interacting with colleagues in the professional sphere, engaging with neighbours in your residential communities, or even forging connections through digital platforms and social media, we've grown to be accustomed to a subtle sense of disconnection although we appear close. Spouses don't know each other as they ought to, parents are strangers to their children, team leaders and managers are disconnected from their teams and even the relationships with friends, both old and new, are being strained. There's a sense that something vital, something deeply human, may be missing and slipping through the digital cracks.

This is the world we find ourselves in today, the head, representing intellectual expertise, strategic thinking, and a continuous quest for knowledge as well as the hand, symbolising technical know-how and the day-to-day operations often take centre stage. But right before our eyes, we have inadvertently left behind the very essence that defines our humanity—the heart.

This neglect has given rise to a host of concerns, from the subtle flicker of disengagement in the workplace to the passive attitude of dissatisfaction. Alarming levels of toxicity have surfaced, both in professional and personal spheres alike. Despite the technological advances surrounding us, the prevalence of discontent, disengaged, and, at times, despaired professionals in the modern workplace is undeniable. Sometimes as a professional, you feel the weight of low morale in the workplace, and it appears like your daily grind is draining your motivation. There have been instances when feedback from superiors left you feeling disheartened, and occasional conflicts and misunderstandings with colleagues and loved ones led to a breakdown in communication.

Furthermore, the relentless demands and pressures of work have taken their toll on some, leading to stress and burnout. There are times when coping with setbacks feels like an uphill battle and social interactions are avoided due to the fear of connecting with certain individuals. It is essential to remember that you are not alone in facing these universal hurdles in both your professional and personal lives. The good news is that there exists a methodology, a roadmap capable of helping you navigate these obstacles while harmoniously integrating the head and the hand without neglecting the heart. I'll walk you through this framework in this book. Whether you are a seasoned leader, an up-and-coming professional, or simply an individual seeking to enhance your emotional well-being, this journey is tailored to resonate with you.

In an era dominated by automation, artificial intelligence, and digital transformation, it is imperative to recognise that working with the heart remains an indispensable aspect of our lives. Harvard Business Review's extensive research reveals a crucial fact that teams with higher average emotional intelligence scores consistently outperform those with lower scores by a significant margin. Yet, despite this compelling evidence, mental health concerns are on the rise, and the rate of disengagement in today's workplace is alarming. The quality of human relationships has dwindled, becoming a distant memory.

While it may be tempting to overlook the significance of emotional intelligence in favour of other metrics that emphasize intellectual and technical prowess, it is essential to realise that the cost of emotional imbalance is not merely reflected in spreadsheets and profit margins. This cost extends far beyond the boardroom, affecting lives and well-being; hearts are involved. You don't need to wait that long. In the chapters ahead, we embark on a transformative journey to rediscover the heart. We venture deep into the art of emotional intelligence, where the head and hand work in harmony but never at the expense of the heart. It's a journey that promises not only professional success but also personal growth.

Through this exploration, you will find healing, rejuvenation, wholeness, and wisdom. You will learn to build exceptional human connections, nurture relationships, and forge lasting, memorable business and professional networks. This book transcends the realm of a mere guide; it serves as a clarion call to action, imploring professionals, leaders, and executives to reignite the profound significance of emotional intelligence in an era where technology and metrics often overshadow the human element. It beckons you to create workplaces that are not only efficient but also compassionate, environments where individuals are not viewed as mere cogs in a machine but as cherished contributors to a shared vision.

As we navigate this landscape together, keep one immutable truth in mind: your emotions are ever in motion, but you are the driver behind the steering wheel. You possess the power to steer your journey, leverage the immense force of your emotions, and create a home, a workplace, a neighbourhood, and an environment where hearts aren't lost but found.

I am immensely grateful for the opportunity to have trained a couple of organisations on emotional intelligence, utilising my bespoke methodology that harmonises the head and the hand without losing the heart. The transformation witnessed has been nothing short of remarkable. It is my sincere hope that you, too, will experience the same profound impact that my physical and virtual participants have encountered as you progress through this book. This will equip you with the practical tools, exercises, and invaluable insights, all designed to empower you to master the delicate art of working in harmony with your intellect, skill, and emotion.

"E-motions" is a transformative guide that equips you with the tools to master your emotions, enhance your mental well-being, and foster meaningful connections, ultimately leading you to a fulfilling life, with peace of mind, emotional resilience, healing, and happiness at its core.

I extend a warm welcome to you as we embark together on a new era of professional and personal growth.

Chapter 1
My Emotion is in Motion And I'm the Driver

"Life is a highway. You ride it or it rides you."
- Nikita Khrushchev

Back in 2004 as a teenager, we were on the road heading out as a family; my mum was driving while we chatted behind as children. It was just after church and my mum thought about taking us out for lunch. Earlier that day in church, we had the Foursquare Sunday School Rally and I did so well, representing the children's church in my Bible recitations. The same with my sisters. So it was that excitement my mum had when she decided to take us out and celebrate us. Less than a kilometre when we connected with the highway, we were to make a U-turn. But just before the turn, another vehicle from nowhere hit our Nissan Sunny red saloon car. All I remembered was that the vehicle that hit us made a 360° spin on the highway, and then it came to a halt. We were all in shock and at the same time most grateful to God for our safety. Supernaturally, both cars eventually balanced with no hurt and then we proceeded on our journey. In your highway of life, many situations will happen like ours bound to kick you off track and throw away your emotional balance, you must focus on what is within your locus of control. While you can't determine the emotional balance of other road users, you can determine yours and build more resilience. Always remember that you have an unseen emotional vehicle, with you as the driver as you navigate through the journey of life.

Picture life as a vast, interconnected network of highways, each leading to different paths and offering diverse experiences. It's a journey that's exhilarating, challenging, and often surprising. Just as a driver encounters unexpected roadblocks, detours, and changing weather conditions, we too encounter a myriad of emotions on our life's journey. From the euphoria of achievement to the frustration of setbacks, from the warmth of love to the chill of disappointment, emotions are an integral part of our human experience. We find ourselves at a crossroads, making choices that impact not only our journey but also the lives of those around us. Just as a driver must make decisions about which route to take, we must navigate our emotional landscape, choosing how we react to the world around us.

As long as you're a human, you are on this highway and your

journey through life will come with several emotions. In the words of Oliver Goldsmith, "Life is a journey that must be travelled no matter how bad the roads and accommodations." Some emotions may want to drive you off your lane, some others will help you remain on course, you can't choose the emotions but you can choose your response. Like IdleHearts will say, "Life is like a road. It has bumps, cracks, and obstacles, but in the end, it gets you somewhere." Where you get to must be determined ahead of time; if you leave the destination to chance, you may get to where you didn't bargain. This is why you hear some persons say things like, "Oh, I didn't mean to, I don't know what came over me," etc.

Motion and Inertia

Allow me to indulge you with my high school fascination with Newton's laws of motion. I drew lots of lessons from the first law, even beyond the boarders of physics. The first law states, "Every object will remain at rest or in uniform motion in a straight line unless compelled to change its state by the action of an external force." In the same vein, we can liken ourselves to objects in motion, each carrying a unique emotional state. These emotional states are like the forces that dictate our actions, reactions, and overall well-being. Just as Newton's law suggests, we tend to remain in our emotional states—be they positive or negative—unless something compels us to change.

Think about those moments when you or someone you know has remained stuck in a particular emotional state for example, indifference, unforgiveness, grief, rage, boredom, or depression. It's as if there's an invisible force making it difficult to break free from such negative emotional states. Ponder on this: Why do certain emotions persist, especially the negative ones? Why does someone grapple with feelings of depression, disengagement, or discontent in their professional life? This is where the concept of emotional inertia comes into play. Emotional inertia refers to the tendency to stay in a current emotional state unless an external force—knowledge in this case—acts upon it. This is the reason why people can linger in unhappiness, unable to move toward more positive emotions, without intervention to compel a change. If you look back to Newton's first law, we find a clue—a force is required to maintain the status quo of a predominant emotion or otherwise. Conversely, when you witness a colleague who manages to sustain positive emotions despite challenges, it's also due to a force—the force of knowledge.

When you look closely, you'll see that emotional inertia is the degree to which emotional states are resistant to change.[1] I want you to come to that point of clarity with the courage to break the inertia and build momentum; you must know that your emotion is in motion, but you are the driver. The term "emotion" is derived from the Latin word, *'emovere'* meaning to move, move out or move through. Essentially, emotion propels motion. As aptly described by Jacqui Butler, an emotion is a prompt from us, to us, to move.[2] However, it's essential to remember that you are the one in control, the driver behind the steering wheel. Equipped with the right skills and training, you can navigate and steer your emotions effectively, regardless of the challenges they present. Can we do this together, now personalise this affirmation and say to yourself, "My emotion is in motion and I am the driver!" Say it one more time, "My emotion is in motion and I am the driver." Fantastic! Thank you for doing this. Let me show you how practical this can get: imagine an individual who is in a toxic or unfulfilling courtship relationship. Despite the red flags of emotional turmoil and unhappiness experienced, such a person finds it challenging to leave the relationship. They remain in this emotional state of unhappiness because the fear of change and the unknown exerts a powerful emotional inertia.

An individual for example, stuck in a dead-end job that provides no fulfilment or growth opportunities, experiencing chronic stress and burnout may remain in this emotional state Mondays through Fridays due to financial security or fear of change. The emotional inertia keeps them from pursuing a more fulfilling career path. Sometimes, it could be struggling with emotional trauma or unresolved issues of years past; unknowingly, such a person may remain trapped in these negative emotional states for many more years to come except intercepted by an external force such as going for life coaching sessions, therapy, and counselling sessions to break free from such emotional inertia, facilitating healing and personal growth.

What could be that emotional inertia for you? What has held you back? What have you been resisting to change over the years? In the next chapter, I'll show you how to grow in self-awareness of any predominant emotions you have, especially those that are harmful when prolonged. But here's the exciting part: knowledge serves as the superior force that can compel a change in an emotional state. Just as an external force can alter an object's motion, knowledge has the power to shift one's emotional trajectory. When you're driving on the highway and you receive superior guidance from your maps, you follow through with such guidance, even if you have a way to navigate differently. Before you picked up this book to read, you felt something. Maybe it was curiosity, prompting you to explore this body of work, or perhaps it was indifference, driving you to skim through and see what new insights might be gleaned. Here's a fundamental truth: "Your emotion is always in motion, but you're the driver."

The Steering Control

When I started learning how to drive, like every other learner, I was in an initial zone of conscious incompetence, and soon, over time and practice, I transitioned into another zone of conscious competence. What does this mean? I remember how, as a learner, I couldn't look away for a split second to the left, nor could I glance to the right. I'm sure you had a similar experience. For some people, it was quite embarrassing, as more experienced drivers possibly looked down on you and sneered at your efforts.

Why did this happen, you might wonder? It was all because of the way you held the steering wheel. Your navigation around bends and between lanes felt mechanical and lacked seamlessness and smoothness. But that's perfectly fine, don't you think? That's exactly what a learner should do. No child starts to run and jump without first crawling, stumbling, and taking those wobbly first steps. It's the same with your emotions. As the driver of your emotional journey, you have to hold the steering wheel firmly during this early stage of mastering emotional intelligence until the time comes when this skill becomes second nature to you. What does this imply, you may ask?

This implies that as you embark on the journey to master emotional intelligence, especially in the early stages, it's entirely natural to experience a sense of conscious competence. You're actively aware of your emotions, and how they influence your thoughts and actions, and you're making a deliberate effort to steer them in a desired direction. Just as you need time and practice to develop the muscle memory and instincts for smooth and confident driving, you'll need to invest effort and time into understanding and regulating your emotions. It's like practising those first parallel parking attempts until they become second nature.

As you progress on this journey, you'll find that managing your emotions becomes more seamless and automatic. It evolves from conscious competence to unconscious competence. Just like when you've become an experienced driver who effortlessly navigates busy highways and narrow lanes, you'll become adept at handling a wide range of emotions and situations without having to consciously think about it. So, while it's entirely normal to start with a firm grip on the emotional steering wheel, know that with dedication, practice, and the right knowledge, you can eventually steer your emotional journey with grace and ease. In the chapters ahead, we'll explore the strategies and tools to help you transition from conscious competence to unconscious competence in mastering emotional intelligence.

The steering wheel in your hands symbolises your emotional control centre, and your destination is a place where peace of mind, good mental health, joy, and harmonious relationships await. Just as a skilled driver adjusts their grip on the wheel to navigate curves and stay on course, you can also learn to steer your emotions in the direction of your desired outcomes. This requires active engagement and control because your emotional journey is not passive. Just as a driver must focus on the road ahead to avoid accidents and stay on course, you must remain vigilant and intentional in managing your emotions.

On the journey of life, while you can't control the road, you can control the steering wheel. In a typical vehicle, the steering wheel is stiff and unyielding when the car is at a standstill. It is only when the wheels are in motion that it becomes responsive, allowing you to guide the vehicle in your chosen direction. Similarly, in everyday affairs, you are in constant motion. You meet people, engage in conversations, and create memories along the way. It's a dynamic journey, and you are the driver. However, to truly make the most of this journey, you need to be skilful at steering the wheel of your emotions in the direction you desire.

You see, life is full of interactions with others. It's like you're on a busy highway with lanes of varying speeds and behaviours.

Every person you meet is like a vehicle in one of those lanes. You can't control how they drive, just as you can't control the actions of others in your lives. But here's where your power lies: in steering your emotional responses. When someone unexpectedly veers into your lane, acting in a way you didn't anticipate, you can't control their actions. However, you can control your response rather than reacting, steering your emotional state in the direction that serves you best. For instance, rather than reacting hastily with frustration or anger when faced with an unrefined or challenging person, you can choose a different path. You can steer your emotions toward patience, understanding, and empathy. By doing so, you not only enhance our well-being but also contribute to a more harmonious journey for everyone involved. I'll share more on this in the subsequent chapters. But remember, while you can't control the road, you have the incredible power to control the steering wheel of your emotions. It's in your hands to chart your course, respond thoughtfully to unexpected challenges, and make the journey a fulfilling and meaningful one. The road is unpredictable, but your emotional steering is your compass to a smoother ride. Now, over to you.

The Fluidity of Emotions

Emotions are transient, temporal, and short-lived. It is often said, "Never make a permanent decision based on a temporary emotion." This affirms the inherently fluid nature of emotions. Consider the emotions you experience daily, they can range from joy when receiving good news to frustration during a traffic jam. Emotions are not static entities that remain fixed in one state. They are dynamic, ever-changing, and responsive to our thoughts, experiences, and circumstances. Dr. Niyi Borire, award-winning neurologist, and neuroscience researcher noted that humans experience a wide range of emotions throughout the day, with some estimates indicating as many as 150 different emotions in a single hour. Ongoing research in psychology and neuroscience continually advances comprehension of this intricate aspect of human psychology.

While you may not consciously recognise every emotion you experience in a given hour, your brain is continually processing and responding to a rich array of emotional stimuli, thus the importance of emotional intelligence and self-awareness. The complexity and diversity of human emotional experiences are also reiterated in the study conducted by Fredrickson, and Losada, who noted that people tend to experience positive emotions approximately 2.5 times more frequently than negative emotions. However, it's worth noting that individuals also encounter instances where they simultaneously experience both positive and negative emotions relatively frequently.[2]

According to research in the field of psychology and neuroscience, our emotional experiences are influenced by various factors, including external stimuli, internal thoughts, and past experiences. Our brains continuously process this information, leading to a dynamic and constantly shifting emotional state.

Similarly, Dr. Lisa Feldman Barrett, a distinguished neuroscientist, suggests that our brains construct emotions based on a variety of inputs, and this construction can lead to a wide array of emotional states. These emotional shifts are like the changing weather patterns, unpredictable and constantly evolving. Understanding the fluidity of emotions is a fundamental aspect of emotional intelligence.

Imagine a day when you woke up feeling particularly cheerful and motivated. Your emotional state resembled the clear skies of a bright morning. As you went about your day, a series of challenging events unfolded, triggering frustration, disappointment, and even anger. Your emotional landscape transformed, much like the sudden onset of a cloudy sky. However, by evening, things settled, and you found yourself once again in a calm and content state. Emotions can shift dramatically within a short span, influenced by external circumstances, thoughts, and interactions. And like they say, "The only constant thing is change." If you don't master the fluidity of emotions, you may make irreversible decisions based on temporary emotions.

For instance, in the heat of anger, an individual sends a hurtful message to a colleague. Later, when the emotional storm has passed, they deeply regret their actions. The decision to send that message was based on a temporary emotion, but the consequences can linger. Studies show that individuals with higher emotional intelligence are better equipped to manage their emotions, leading to improved mental health and well-being. The ability to pause, reflect, and respond rather than react impulsively is a skill in emotional intelligence. By understanding that even the most intense emotions are temporary, we gain the ability to navigate them with greater foresight.

Steering Your Emotions Toward Your Desired Destination

"Life is 10% what happens to us and 90% how we react to it." – Charles R. Swindoll

As a driver on the highway, the most important task among others is to continue to steer the wheel to a desired course. When you choose to navigate to another lane, you use the steering wheel; when you're climbing up an interchange, you use the steering wheel; when you're parking, you use the steering wheel; almost everything is done using the steering wheel. Fundamentally, your words and self-talk are the steering wheels of your emotions; I will expound on this in chapters six and seven.

Has anyone asked you this question in recent times or have you overhead it from a conversation, "Please take good care of yourself..." I have heard it several times; it's either someone is telling another person who is on bed rest or sick leave or who needs some form of medical care. And that's where it ends. I haven't heard anyone say, "Please take good care of your mind." In other words, the former details the concerns for one's physical well-being while the latter is more concerned about one's emotional health and mental health. Do you also take care of your mind? Or just your body? Do you take care of your emotions? I encourage you to observe closely and extend your empathy and care to one another beyond the borders of physical health only.

As a professional, you encounter an array of emotions daily that shape your experiences and outcomes. However, what can set you apart is your ability to master the steering wheel of your emotions, guiding you towards a destination of your choosing, regardless of the road you're on. Imagine a scenario where a colleague, in a moment of heated tension, speaks rudely to you. This interaction is an emotional crossroads, a relationship with others that triggers an immediate surge of your feelings. What do you do? Do you just swerve or leave the steering because someone angered you? And then you go ahead and hit the emotional vehicle of that colleague? Or perhaps you received a stinker mail from your manager, who happens not to be emotionally intelligent at the time. And because of that, your eyeballs pop out upon reading the mail, your heartbeat increases, riled up as you read it again and your breathing intensifies, what do you do? Instantly your mood changes like a sharp bend on a road. How do you continue to steer your emotional vehicle rightly? On the other hand, if it's your birthday or a wedding anniversary— automatically, that circumstance will evoke a unique emotional response. Most likely, you will be happy, grateful, and optimistic, for a prolonged part of that day. As you read various messages sent to you, you remain in the emotional state of gratitude to God for life and wellness as you anticipate the best year yet. That's the power of circumstances; they can alter one's emotions positively or negatively. Amidst all of these, here's the fundamental truth: you possess the power to steer your emotional journey. You can work with the head (knowledge) and the hand (skills) without losing the heart (emotions). That's what emotional intelligence does, it equips you to identify the emotional signposts that punctuate your professional journey, enabling you to make informed choices about how to respond. It empowers you to steer your emotions with purpose and finesse, ensuring they align harmoniously with your desired destination.

Visualise your emotional vehicle and see yourself in the driver's seat, with your hands on the steering wheel. Inside the vehicle are other spheres of your life, your career – your professional life, your spouse – your marital life, your parenting –your children, your family – your siblings and relatives, your mentors, friends, and neighbours – your social life, these persons are all in your emotional vehicle. The road ahead may not always be smooth, yet, your emotional steering wheel is the tool that empowers you to navigate the intricate interchanges of your diverse relationships, driving to your desired destination. Talking about your desired destination, have you thought about what it takes to be a truly exceptional leader? What distinguishes a professional who not only excels in their work but also maintains unwavering ethical standards, skillfully manages burnout and overwhelm, and harmoniously interacts with people from diverse cultures? The answer lies in mastering Emotional Intelligence (EI).

Daniel Goleman, a renowned psychologist known for his groundbreaking work in popularising the concept of emotional intelligence defines it as the art of understanding one's feelings, developing empathy for others, and regulating emotions in a way that enriches our lives. Emotional intelligence is the key to fostering deep connections, both personally and professionally. The essence of EI lies in recognising emotions, comprehending their profound impact, and harnessing that knowledge to steer your thoughts and behaviours in a positive direction, as explained by Justin J. Bariso. It's the compass that guides us through the complexity of human interaction. Here's a fascinating insight, according to the World Economic Forum, Emotional Intelligence ranks among the top 10 vital skills for the future workforce. By cultivating EI, you equip yourself to thrive in an ever-evolving professional landscape.

Maya Angelou once wisely remarked, "At the end of the day, people won't remember what you said or did, they'll remember how you made them feel." Imagine a workplace culture where happiness and well-being are at the forefront. It's a culture that prioritises not only your intellectual prowess but also your emotional health, as recognised by the U.S. Department of Health & Human Services. There are many benefits to honing your EI skills. From enhancing your career potential to achieving life harmony, often called work-life balance, to experiencing greater job satisfaction, and boosting your overall productivity. Imagine confidently managing demanding clients and nurturing cohesive relationships with your colleagues and team members. These are the benefits among others for mastering emotional intelligence. This is not only for professionals and team members but also managers and executives. As Daniel Goleman rightly said, "CEOs are hired for their intellect and business expertise - and fired for a lack of emotional intelligence." Everyone needs this skill not as a one-off acquisition, but as a lifelong journey of development.

Talking about skill, imagine the driver of a truck and the driver of a car; although they have the same skill of driving, they are not at the same skill level. There are other intricacies required to drive a long vehicle that isn't required for a four-wheel vehicle. Skill level differs. The skill level required for emotional intelligence as a team member is different from the one required as a manager. The one required as an unmarried young adult is different from the one required as a married adult and a parent. My joy is to see you grow in skill levels as you continue the immersion of this experience. The desired destination is now crystal clear: peace of mind, emotional and mental well-being, and of course, harmony across your relationships. As we delve into the mechanics of emotional intelligence, fasten your seat belt as we advance this journey, mastering your emotional states, learning to regulate them, and building stronger relationships. Remember that you possess the power to overcome emotional inertia and steer your emotional state in the direction you desire.

Highest Learning Points

Take a moment to jot down and highlight the key insights and lessons that resonated with you most in this chapter.

Most Pressing Action Points

Take a moment to note down the key decisions and actions you would take based on the insights gained from this chapter.

Chapter 2
Why I Drive the Way I Do

"Knowing yourself is the beginning of all wisdom." – Aristotle

Imagine this scenario: a driver on the highway, seemingly oblivious to the rules of the road, swerving recklessly in and out of lanes. What thoughts cross your mind in such moments? Do you wonder about the reasons behind their erratic behaviour, whether it's due to intoxication, drowsiness, or something else entirely? I once saw a video where a driver lost control, veering into oncoming traffic at a frightening speed. A police officer conducting a roadside stop-and-check interrogation narrowly escaped a potentially devastating accident.

Every driver on the highway has their unique approach and skill level. Some choose to overtake based on their perception of another driver's inattentiveness, while others make unfortunate calculations that lead to highway accidents. Now, let's apply this analogy to our personal lives. If left uncontrolled, our emotions can drive us haphazardly, steering us away from the path of rational actions and responses. What can be done to avoid emotional "accidents"? As a driver, I've encountered moments of drowsiness behind the wheel, which is why I prefer to have a companion in the vehicle to keep me alert. Often, my spouse accompanies me, and our engaging conversations serve as a valuable distraction.

It's equally important to understand why you drive the way you do on the highway of emotions. Imagine if, as a professional, you had a profound understanding of why you react to certain situations in specific ways. This knowledge can empower you to master your emotional journey, ensuring you stay on the right path. If you know what causes burnout, for example, then you can better handle and master that aspect. Think about it.

One of the ways to do this is to pay attention to your emotional state. Recall that emotions are transient, as such, you can have several emotions within a few hours. Awareness is the beginning of help. Roger Ebert succinctly captured it, "Your intellect may be confused, but your emotions will never lie to you." Sometime back, I got a pool of email replies after I had sent out a mail to my subscribers, checking on them. Rather than the stereotypical question of, "How are you?"

Here were the questions I asked and I want you to pause and respond to them as well.

1. What's been on your mind lately?

2. What has been the highlight of this month so far?

3. Is there anything you'd like to talk about?

4. Is there something you're currently working on or excited about that you'd like to share?

5. What's a recent accomplishment you're proud of?

6. How can I support you right now?

7. What are you looking forward to in the coming weeks or months?

What are your responses, please pause and do this exercise in your journal. This is the beginning of your journey into self-awareness.

The Journey of Self-Awareness

"To know thyself is the beginning of wisdom."
— Socrates

What am I feeling right now? What would I like to feel ideally? What do others feel? How do I want others to feel while interacting with them? This is the essence of self-awareness. It's the ability to recognise the emotions that drive you at any given moment and to understand them. After all, you can only respond to what you're aware of. Imagine you're driving, and your windshield fogs up due to unexpected weather conditions. What's your immediate action? You press the button on your dashboard to clear the mist on the screen. Why? Because you're aware of the situation and you understand what needs to be done. Nathaniel Branden's words ring true: 'The first step toward change is awareness. The second step is acceptance.' Change begins with recognising the aspects of your predominant emotions that require transformation, and acceptance is the bridge that allows you to navigate that journey.

Your words are powerful no doubt, and like I shared earlier, they are your steering control, but if you are not aware of the predominant words you use in your daily conversations, you may not be able to improve and use them wisely. Like Yogi Bhajan rightly said, "You are very powerful, provided you know how powerful you are."

In essence, self-awareness is the foundation upon which emotional intelligence is built; it empowers you to not only understand yourself but also to empathise with others, creating a ripple effect of positive change. According to a study published in the Journal Europe's Journal of Psychology, individuals with high self-awareness tend to experience lower levels of stress and higher levels of life satisfaction.[1]

Think of your self-awareness as the rear-view mirror of your emotional vehicle. It provides you with a clear perspective on your past emotional experiences, helping you navigate your present and future with greater insight. Simultaneously, imagine self-awareness as the dashboard of your emotional vehicle, it provides you with real-time information about your emotions and behaviours.

Understanding your emotional vehicle and why you drive the way you do is the first step toward mastering the art of emotional intelligence. Self-awareness doesn't just help you to understand your emotions; it also empowers you to make conscious choices and adapt your behaviours. With this, you can make more informed decisions that align with your values and goals, and recognise how your emotions affect your interactions with others, leading to better communication and deeper connections. Most importantly, by understanding your emotional triggers and patterns, you can work on areas that require improvement and embark on a journey of self-development.

Cultivating Self-Awareness

> *"Your emotions make you human. Even the unpleasant ones have a purpose. Don't lock them away. If you ignore them, they just get louder and angrier." – Sabaa Tahir*

Self-awareness is a skill that can be nurtured and developed over time. On a personal level, you can set aside dedicated time for introspection, allowing you to reflect on your emotions, actions, and reactions through the practice of journaling. Questions like 'What triggers me to feel this way?' and 'How likely am I to respond?' can guide your reflections. However, it's important to acknowledge that sometimes, you may not remember all your actions and behaviours.

These are your emotional blind spots, similar to the limitations of your car's mirrors while driving. During such moments, seeking external feedback becomes invaluable. You can turn to trusted friends, family members, or colleagues for honest insights into your behaviours and how you come across to others. While striving for self-awareness, it's crucial to remember that you don't have to be overly critical of yourself. Self-awareness isn't synonymous with self-criticism; instead, it's a journey toward self-understanding and personal growth.

Here's an exercise to assist you in integrating self-awareness into your daily life: it's a personal SWOT analysis. Much like its application in business, SWOT stands for Strengths, Weaknesses, Opportunities, and Threats. As an example, consider someone who conducted this analysis and discovered that they excel in team collaboration (a strength) but sometimes struggle with active listening (a weakness). However, they have access to various training opportunities (opportunity), and one potential threat in their context could be a lack of work-life balance.

Now, I encourage you to embark on your personal SWOT analysis. To get started, think about your own life and experiences. By conducting a personal SWOT analysis, you gain valuable insights and awareness into yourself, your environment, and your potential.

Personal SWOT Analysis

Strengths (S):	What are my unique strengths that set me apart from others?

What do I do well?

What unique resources can I draw on? What do others see as my strengths?

Personal SWOT Analysis

Weaknesses (W):	What areas do I feel I need to work on or improve?
	Where do you I fewer resources than others?
	What are others likely to see as weaknesses?

Personal SWOT Analysis

Opportunities (O):	What opportunities can I tap into to further my goals and well-being?
	How can I turn my strengths into opportunities?

Personal SWOT Analysis	
Threats (T):	What external threats, if any, might influence my path?
	What threats do my weaknesses expose me to?

Emotions and Biological Well-being

Professor Carolyn Stern, author of the 'Emotionally Strong Leader,' affirms that "You can be emotional and strong; they are not mutually exclusive. Connecting with the heart of the people you lead is the key to your leadership success." One of the keys to achieving this is to become aware of your emotions, and how you feel at times. You don't have to ignore your feelings. Your goal is not to remain in one particular emotional state, especially if it's not a good one, your goal is to become aware of it in the first place.

As Eckhart Tolle rightly puts it, "Rather than being your thoughts and emotions, be the awareness behind them." There are tons of words to describe your emotions per time, be conscious to pinpoint which is your feeling per time. Do you recall the memorable Malta Guinness TV commercial that brilliantly featured James Brown's 1966 hit 'I Feel Good'? It left a lasting impression on many of us. In that iconic ad, James Brown passionately affirmed his feelings with the catchy lyrics, 'I feel good.' It was a sensational campaign that resonated with audiences. However, it's important to remember that in life, you may not always feel good, and that's perfectly normal.

That doesn't mean all is not good, it does only mean that we will not be in one emotional state. Emotions are fluid and ever-changing, and experiencing a range of emotions is part of being human. The beginning of your mastering of your emotions and your emotional health is knowing how you feel. For example, do you feel happy, heartbroken, positive, confident, grieved, or miserable? Do you feel inspired, hopeful, nervous, insecure, relaxed, loved, desperate, stressed? Or do you feel intimidated, embarrassed, frustrated, confused? How do you feel per time? Excited, optimistic, surprised, disappointed, overwhelmed, sad? Or do you feel cheated, angered, fearful, satisfied, disrespected, uncomfortable, bored?

Scientifically, psychologists have studied closely the interplay of human emotions and human physiology. The physiology of emotions notes that emotions are caused by many biological instincts or urges. Look at a pregnant woman for example, she feels like throwing up, and because of that biological instinct, she feels nauseated and vice-versa. I remember during my wife's first pregnancy, she often felt this way predominantly during her early conception, the usual morning sickness and the thrills of that season.

It was a new phase we needed to grapple with and soon she got better in the second trimester. Paul Ekman further expanded this in his cross-cultural study when he categorised emotions into six main blocks - happiness, sadness, anger, fear, disgust, and surprise noting that they are universal and easily recognisable across cultures.[3] Ekman's research, primarily focused on facial expressions, has shown that these emotions are associated with unique facial muscle movements, making them easily identifiable. Have you noticed that in a person who feels sad, the zygomaticus muscle which is most responsible for smiling is not active?

This validates the connection between emotions and biological well-being. Even though you may see a fake smile, it can't be compared to the original. First within, before without, the desired emotional state must be in place to propel the outward response. This is the purpose of this book, to walk you through mastering your emotional health for personal and professional success. Rats differ from humans in their emotional displays. Unlike humans, rats do not express their emotions through facial expressions, primarily because their emotional responses are not intricately linked to the movement of their facial muscles.

Furthermore, the discrete emotion theory paints a graphic illustration of emotions as distinct colours on a palette noting that emotions are not just a mix but individual and easily recognisable[4]. Even though we feel several emotions almost at the same time or within the same period, the emotionally intelligent professional is the one who can identify all emotions, and respond to them individually, not muddled up. Even when you have mixed feelings, identify the emotions that made you feel that way.

I was training some young adults many years back and I could see everyone in the room. Suddenly, I started to take notice of a particular lady in the room who was not connected to the session; attention wasn't there and she literally wasn't in the class although her body was. Even to my humour, she turned a deaf ear. My prognosis was right, as an emotionally intelligent trainer and teacher; I knew something was wrong. So I walked up to her after I was done and she came along as I walked away. So I asked, "Are you fine...?" She initially gave me the stereotypical response, "Fine." But of course, I knew she wasn't. As I communicated more from a place of trust and empathy, she eventually opened up and told me that, she just had a heartbreak! I empathised and shared some comforting words and followed up through her recovery process. That was the predominant emotion that affected her cognition and devoid her of attention in the class. If this wasn't properly handled, persons like that had gone on to develop that experience as a limiting belief that continued to affect their life's outcome. Yours might have been something else, perhaps you don't eat a particular food, fruit, or beverage because you had an experience growing up and that affected your emotions, and since then, unconsciously it became a limiting belief for you. Your healing has come! I'll show you what to do shortly as we make progress.

But first, ask yourself the following questions whenever you feel a particular emotion:

First, identify the emotion and give it a name;

Go ahead and ask yourself, "Is this how I would love to feel?"

Next, define how you would love to feel

Why would you love to feel that way?

This is self-awareness!

Emotions and Limiting Beliefs

> *"I am not what happened to me, I am what I choose to become." - Carl Gustav Jung*

Not everyone can rightly say this, for some, what happened to them, is still happening in them, let's talk about this. This is the time for someone's emotional healing right time. Come along with

53

me. The truth is your past experiences and emotions can become a foothold, which we call a limiting belief consciously or subconsciously. Then, these limiting beliefs go ahead to influence a person's thoughts, behaviours, and life outcomes. So, you hear people make conclusions and decisions like this, "All men are bad!" "I can't work with this industry again," "I will never travel by air anymore," "I don't take this." You hear categorical statements like, "I can never speak before many people, if they're more than fifty, I can't do it." You hear more statements like, "I can never invest there again," "I will never send my child to that school," "I can never do business with anyone from this region," "I can never use new technology," "I'll never go near tall buildings or cliffs again." The list is endless, "I can never trust someone completely," I'm just not a creative person," "I can never trust people I meet online," "I can never take risks; I've been burned before." The list goes on and on. How can you heal from these and overcome these limiting beliefs?

You must be able to reflect and be aware of the limiting beliefs you've developed knowingly or unknowingly. Then, you can be able to do something about it. Recognising and challenging these beliefs is a crucial step toward personal growth and emotional intelligence. One of the first things I want you to do is to recall, "What experiences and emotions brought about this limiting belief?"

For some people, certain situations happened to them and later became limiting beliefs. For example, if you had a traumatic experience while speaking in public during your school days and you received harsh criticism and faced ridicule from classmates, chances are that such experience could have developed into a deep-seated fear of public speaking and that limiting belief is now hindering your career and personal growth. How about a person who experienced repeated rejection in past romantic relationships and subconsciously developed a belief that "I am unlovable or unworthy of love." This limiting belief has gone ahead to sabotage future relationships unknowingly. A betrayal or deception in a close relationship subconsciously develops a deep-seated limiting belief that people cannot be trusted. And now, there is difficulty in forming new relationships and maintaining existing ones. We call them limiting beliefs because they limit the experiences and outcomes one should achieve in life.

Look at another instance of a person who experienced failure or setback, a failed business venture or a rejection from a dream job, that experience if not properly managed has led to a limiting belief that now instilled a fear of failure and now prevents such a person from taking risks or pursuing new opportunities. In the same vein, someone who has experienced body shaming with negative comments or bullying related to appearance during adolescence can lead to a limiting belief that now significantly impacts self-esteem and relationships. This is the time to resolve all limiting beliefs. Don't let them persist in resisting you, break their hold, and enjoy life to the full as God originally designed.

I know you have buried that issue and you feel this has sorted it, but it hasn't. You don't even want to talk about it again. But deep within you, you still sense fear and unforgiveness. It needs a final solution. "For the thing I greatly feared has come upon me, and what I dreaded has happened to me." [5]

Now, I'll ask you the following questions, please pause and reflect on each deeply; then note down your responses. There is an example after this exercise you may want to look at it first before attempting the exercise. When you're set, you can start. Don't skip this, this is your healing. Let's go:

Identifying My Limiting Beliefs

What negative thoughts and self-talk do I often tell myself? Write them out

What recurring patterns have I noticed that consistently lead to negative outcomes?

What experiences and emotions brought about this?

When was this, around what time of my life did it happen?

Welldone, the conclusion of this exercise is the most important: now let's progress to it: Going forward, how would you want to feel about the identified limiting belief(s)?

Create a positive affirmation that directly contradicts the limiting belief.

Repeat the affirmation daily, for the next twenty-one days. Monitor your thoughts and emotions as you repeat the affirmation. *Write the word, "Done," for the next twenty-one days. One for each day.*

Here is an example to guide you:

Identifying My Limiting Beliefs [Example]

What negative thoughts and self-talk do I often tell myself?
Write them out

"I can't trust anyone; they'll just let me down."

"I'm not good enough for a healthy relationship."

"People will always deceive me."

"I'm better off alone to avoid getting hurt."

What recurring patterns have I noticed that consistently lead to negative outcomes?

"I tend to distance myself from close relationships."

"I become overly suspicious and doubt people's intentions."

"I have difficulty opening up to others emotionally."

"I often self-sabotage potential relationships due to fear."

What experiences and emotions brought about this?

"I was betrayed by my best friend in high school."

"I've had several romantic relationships end in deception."

"I experienced a significant loss of trust during my childhood."

"Emotions like anger, hurt, and sadness have been constant companions."

When was this, around what time of my life did it happen?

"The betrayal by my best friend happened when I was 16."

"I first experienced deception in a romantic relationship in my early 20s."

"These trust issues began during my childhood, around age 10."

"Emotions like anger, hurt, and sadness have been present since adolescence."

Going forward, how would you want to feel about the identified limiting belief(s)?

"I want to feel more open and trusting in my relationships."

"I aspire to have healthier and more fulfilling connections."

"I aim to let go of the fear of betrayal and focus on positive connections."

"I want to feel confident that I can trust others again."

Create a positive affirmation that directly contradicts the limiting belief.

"I am open to trusting others and building meaningful connections."

"I deserve healthy, loving relationships in my life."

"I choose to believe that people can be trustworthy."

"I am worthy of love and trust, and I embrace it."

Repeat the affirmation daily, for the next twenty-one days. Monitor your thoughts and emotions as you repeat the affirmation. *Write the word, "Done," for the next twenty-one days. One for each day.*

Done	Done	Done	Done	Done	Done	Done
Done	Done	Done	Done	Done	Done	Done
Done	Done	Done	Done	Done	Done	Done

Highest Learning Points

Take a moment to jot down and highlight the key insights and lessons that resonated with you most in this chapter.

Most Pressing Action Points

Take a moment to note down the key decisions and actions you would take based on the insights gained from this chapter.

Chapter 3
Driving with Functional Brakes

"Life is 10% what happens to us and 90% how we react to it." - Charles R. Swindoll

One of the blessings of automobiles is the crucial tool called, the brakes! Imagine you couldn't control the motion, that would be a disaster, right? How much more are your emotions? Yes, they're in motion and you are behind the wheel and you have the brakes to control them. Imagine a wife, husband, professional, parent, or grandparent driving on the highways of life without brakes. Such persons run into ditches frequently, they don't get along with others easily and they experience bashes and emotional accidents.

Just as brakes are essential for controlling a car's speed and direction, self-regulation is the emotional intelligence brake system that allows you to manage and navigate your emotions effectively. In this chapter, we'll delve deep into the art of driving with functional brakes in the realm of emotional intelligence.

The Power of Self-Regulation

First, you need to master the art of regulating your own emotions before you can help others. Daniel Goleman puts it this way, "The more you can regulate your own emotions, the more you can influence the emotions of others." You will not always have positive emotions, what do you do at those moments of negative emotions? According to Publilius Syrus, "Anyone can hold the helm when the sea is calm." But that's not in emotional intelligence. You must be able to self-regulate both in calm moments and more importantly in raging moments.

Self-regulation is the ability to manage your emotions, impulses, and behaviours in a way that aligns with your long-term goals and values. It's the emotional brake that allows you to stay on course, even when the road gets bumpy. Just as a skilled driver adjusts their speed and applies the brakes when necessary, self-regulation empowers you to navigate the ups and downs of life with grace and composure. This is very important just as a vehicle cannot survive without brakes. In life, self-regulation is your emotional brake pedal, allowing you to respond thoughtfully rather than react impulsively.

Similarly, it is not just about the safety of a vehicle on the road to have functional brakes, but much more for the safety and benefit of other road users. In the same vein, think of emotions as such contagious forces, that can affect and infect others. Don't transfer bad energy, mirror positive emotions. You have a remarkable ability to shape not only our own experiences but also the world around us. It's not just about how you feel in the moment; it's about the ripple effect that your emotions create, extending far beyond the boundaries of your hearts and minds. If you zoom in on the people closest to you – your family, your friends, your colleagues, and your loved ones, you will notice that these are the individuals who are most susceptible to the contagious nature of your emotions. They are the first responders to your emotional energy, whether they realise it or not. It's like a feedback loop of feelings.

When you're overjoyed, your loved ones become even happier, and when you're distressed, their worry deepens. This amplification effect is one reason why emotional intelligence is so crucial in our interactions. In the words of John Mayer, emotional intelligence is a way of recognising, understanding, and choosing how we think, feel, and act. Understanding the contagious nature of emotions is a call to responsibility. In the words of Marshall B. Rosenberg, "We are dangerous when we are not conscious of our responsibility for how we behave, think, and feel." Your emotions have the power to uplift, inspire, and heal, but they can also sow seeds of discord and negativity if left unchecked. So, the next time you find yourself in the embrace of a powerful emotion, take a moment to consider its potential impact on those around you.

Recognise that your emotional energy can be a force for good, a source of comfort, and a catalyst for positive change or otherwise. Embrace the power you have to create a ripple effect of positivity and understanding, not only within your own heart but throughout the lives of those you touch. Don't hesitate to seek support from a trusted friend, mentor, or therapist when you need guidance in managing your emotions.

Cultivating Self-Regulation: The Benefits of Self-Regulation

"Emotional self-regulation is not about suppressing emotions; it's about understanding them."

In my driving history, two vivid instances stand out where I found myself in a bumper-to-bumper traffic scenario. In both cases, I can recall being slightly distracted, my mind wandering elsewhere, when suddenly, I heard the unmistakable sound of a minor collision. Fortunately, there were no serious damages on either occasion. It's moments like these that make you appreciate the value of functional brakes when you're navigating the complexities of traffic. After all, without proper brakes, you'd be at a heightened risk of colliding with other vehicles on the road. Just as functional brakes are crucial for avoiding vehicular collisions, self-regulation is paramount for steering clear of emotional collisions in challenging situations. Let me elaborate on this connection.

In the instances I mentioned earlier, my vehicle's brakes were indeed functional. However, my momentary distraction and lack of focus led to those minor bumps. It wasn't that I lacked the means to control my vehicle; rather, I failed to exercise that control effectively in those moments. Similarly, in emotional intelligence, you possess the tools and capacity for self-regulation. It's within your grasp to manage and navigate your emotional responses, much like operating the brakes of a car. However, when you allow yourself to be carried away by powerful emotions or fail to apply self-regulation effectively, you risk emotional collisions. Whether it's a challenging situation in your workplace or at home, it's like navigating through heavy traffic, filled with potential stressors and triggers. Self-regulation is your emotional brake system in these moments. It enables you to modulate your reactions, maintain composure, and make thoughtful choices in your responses.

When you neglect self-regulation, it's like letting your emotions take the wheel, potentially leading to emotional collisions that could have been avoided. Self-regulation isn't just about avoiding emotional outbursts; it's a powerful tool that can enhance your well-being and relationships. Self-regulation allows you to think clearly, enabling better decision-making, especially in high-pressure situations. When you control your emotional reactions, you foster healthier connections with others, leading to improved relationships both at work and in your personal life.

Heads up, not every driver on the road is as skilled as you are! In the same vein, be prepared to encounter individuals with varying levels of emotional intelligence; anticipate the diversity of drivers and conditions. Just as you anticipate encountering different drivers, also expect to come across diverse emotional situations and conditions. Being a skilled driver isn't solely about safely reaching your destination; it's about gracefully navigating the journey while maintaining control. Similarly, self-regulation in emotional intelligence serves as your tool for traversing life's highways, mitigating emotional collisions, and ensuring a smoother ride. Much like you would anticipate different road conditions and prepare your response ahead of time, emotional intelligence equips you with the ability to foresee and manage various emotional scenarios. Just as you adapt your driving style to suit the road ahead, self-regulation enables you to adjust your emotional responses to suit the circumstances you encounter.

Everyone can Evolve

I often hear people use phrases like "That's just who I am," "I've always been this way," or "I can't change; it's my nature." Similarly, some boldly state, " I'm just being myself," unknowingly to them, these words often reveal the presence of limiting beliefs. If you've diligently completed the exercise I shared in chapter two, you'll likely come to a profound realisation over time: "Everyone can evolve!" Here's a story of David, he joined my life harmony coaching program in 2021, and at the close of the year, here was his testimonial:

"At the end of 2021, I was so disturbed about how to balance, my spiritual, business, academic life, financial, and marital life together without having to rob/pause one for the other. I was also looking forward to finding my career path, solving my financial crisis, and living a fulfilling life. The courses have shaped me and guided me to live a holistic life, a life where all areas of life have a common goal. I love the way the modules were arranged, they were arranged in the right sense of learning, just like A before B and B before C. What an amazing journey with Dr. Abraham. He held our hands throughout the journey, giving room for clarity. The journey has been amazing, with lots of encounters, lots of discovery, lots of attention, and lots of intentional decisions. The experiences from the coaching call can't be summarised. Dr. Abraham is a man of purpose, a real exemplary coach, following him is like following the brightness of light because the more I move closer, the brighter he becomes. I have also become light by following him, people now want to come around me, they want me to speak, they want me to share ideas based on what I have learned, and they want to see my approach to life situations. Dr. Abraham has taught me well."

You also can evolve. Self-regulation is a skill that can be developed and refined over time. I once worked with a senior colleague who previously had a phlegmatic personality but easily got angry. I'm aware of this because of an outburst I once experienced with her. However, years later, I have observed a 360-degree change in her leadership. You don't need to wait till an emotional outburst before you self-regulate. What leads to outbursts? An outburst is an explosive release of emotion, mostly negative. The answer often lies in bottled emotions, likened to a ticking time bomb, patiently waiting for the right trigger; unchecked weaknesses soon translate to an outburst. What can you do?

Here's an exercise I recommend for you to do:

To do this exercise, look at your previous personal SWOT analysis, transfer your responses under the 'Weaknesses' section, and insert them under the emotions column in this Self-regulation

Worksheet. An example has been done in the first row.

Self-regulation Worksheet

Emotions

What are those emotions that have currently gone out of your control and you know you need to tame them so you can thrive better with people?

Impatience

Triggers

What triggers me to feel like this? What are the stressors?

Waiting in long lines, traffic jams, slow internet connection

Reaction

What has been my default reaction in the past?

Becoming irritable, tapping fingers, sighing loudly

Response & Control

What can I do to control this particular emotion/feeling so I don't act rashly?

To control impatience, I can practice deep breathing techniques when faced with triggers like waiting in lines or traffic. I can remind myself that impatience won't make the situation any better and try to find something productive or enjoyable to do while waiting.

Now, you can go ahead and use the Self-regulation worksheet to design how you can better respond to your emotions, rather than reacting. I've provided three blank copies; use each worksheet for each emotion you want to better regulate.

Self-regulation Worksheet (1)

Emotions

What are those emotions that have currently gone out of your control and you know you need to tame them so you can thrive better with people?

Triggers

What triggers me to feel like this? What are the stressors?

Reaction

What has been my default reaction in the past?

Response & Control

What can I do to control this particular emotion/feeling so I don't act rashly?

Self-regulation Worksheet (2)

Emotions

What are those emotions that have currently gone out of your control and you know you need to tame them so you can thrive better with people?

Triggers

What triggers me to feel like this? What are the stressors?

Reaction

What has been my default reaction in the past?

Response & Control

What can I do to control this particular emotion/feeling so I don't act rashly?

Self-regulation Worksheet (3)

Emotions

What are those emotions that have currently gone out of your control and you know you need to tame them so you can thrive better with people?

Triggers

What triggers me to feel like this? What are the stressors?

Reaction

What has been my default reaction in the past?

Response & Control

What can I do to control this particular emotion/feeling so I don't act rashly?

Expressing Regulated Emotion

Maturity is largely about the ability to take charge of one's emotions, especially how we express them. The proof of self-regulation is the expression of your emotions. "Can't I be myself?" No, you can't! Self-regulated people can't. But here is what you can do, you can be your regulated self. As succinctly captured by Rebecca T. Dickson, a member of the Forbes Coaches Council, "You — and only you — are in control of your reactions and emotions. Once you realise that, you can begin to know yourself on a much deeper level. And then you can begin attracting the right audience for your business and impact them in the best ways."

A self-regulated person expresses feelings in the most appropriate and guarded way. This art of emotional finesse can be transformative in both personal and professional spheres. Nawal Mustafa, a seasoned clinical neuropsychologist offers practical strategies for mastering self-regulation in the face of various emotional challenges. For instance, when feeling overwhelmed by stress, Mustafa suggests shifting your focus to what you can control while consciously letting go of what is beyond your sphere of influence. When loneliness creeps in, she recommends connecting with loved ones through video calls or arranging meetings, nurturing the human connection that is essential for emotional well-being.

Moreover, when confronted with a daunting workload, her advice is to jot down your tasks and prioritise them based on importance. By tackling one task at a time, you can regain a sense of control and manage your responsibilities more effectively.

Additionally, in moments when you doubt your abilities and feel not good enough, Mustafa encourages self-reflection on your strengths and incremental steps toward improving your perceived shortcomings. Perhaps one of the most challenging emotions to navigate is anger. Mustafa wisely advises taking a pause in the heat of the moment, allowing yourself time to regain clarity of thought. This pause enables you to respond to the situation rationally rather than reacting impulsively in the grip of anger.

Incorporating these strategies into your life can lead to a profound transformation in how you express and regulate your emotions. As you embrace self-regulation, you'll discover that it not only enhances your personal growth but also strengthens your relationships and empowers you to impact others positively.

Emotions and Compartmentalisation

Just as the bile of a chicken, if not properly removed, can significantly impact the edibility of the chicken, emotions too can alter your ability to function effectively if not appropriately managed. In architectural design, the concept of compartmentalization refers to the distinct separation of spaces and allocation based on zoning, and functional relationships. So, a residential building for instance has a zone for bedrooms and another for public spaces – living area, and dining. Additionally, the compartmentalisation of spaces helps to prevent the spread of fire in case of a fire outbreak. If fire-prone areas have been compartmentalized with fire-resistant walls, fire doors, and other fire-rated elements, it becomes difficult for the spread of fire, thus enhancing fire safety. It is the same in human emotions, due to the fluidity of emotions, compartmentalisation plays a crucial role in curtailing certain emotions, especially negative ones, and avoiding their spread to other 'spaces.'

Furthermore, as humans, life coaches have unveiled that human expression is divided into these spheres of living: career – your life's work, academics/personal development, recreation/leisure, health, financial, emotional, social, marital and family. Therefore, when negative or distressing emotions begin to take hold in one sphere of life, it's vital to recognise the need to isolate that particular area and work on transitioning away from those emotions. This approach is far more beneficial than allowing those negative emotions to permeate and affect all other areas of our lives.

Compartmentalisation allows you to prevent the spillage of negativity into other areas where positivity and productivity are essential. Because of this, you don't affect your work relationship and delivery because of an unresolved issue between your spouse. As Goi Nasu revealed, "An entire sea of water can't sink a ship unless it gets inside the ship. Similarly, the negativity of the world can't put you down unless you allow it to get inside you."

Moreover, as humans, life coaches have unveiled the life wheel of human expression, which is divided into distinct sectors - spheres of living just like the spaces and rooms in a building. I explain this succinctly in my works on life harmony. These spheres encompass career – your life's work, academics/personal development, recreation/leisure, health, financial well-being, emotional stability, social interactions, spirituality, and the profound bonds of marital and family life. In light of this holistic perspective on human existence, it is paramount to recognise the necessity of isolating a particular area that experiences negative or distressing emotions and diligently work towards transitioning away from those emotions. This approach is far more beneficial than allowing the turmoil of negative emotions to permeate and seep into all other facets of life.

Compartmentalisation, in this context, serves as a valuable tool in maintaining harmony, and preventing the spillage of negativity. You shouldn't permit unresolved emotional issues in one domain to disrupt your overall harmony. A study conducted on emotional regulation, published in the Journal of Psychophysiology highlighted similar strategies for emotion regulation in managing emotions effectively. The study affirmed that by isolating negative emotions, individuals can regain control and prevent the contamination of other facets of their lives (Gross, 2002).[1]

Researchers like Susan David, in her work on emotional agility, emphasise the importance of recognising and managing emotions in various life domains to promote well-being and success.[2] For instance, the ability to address and resolve an issue with your spouse without allowing it to negatively impact your performance and relationships at work is a testament to effective compartmentalisation. So, just as the bile is meticulously removed from a chicken to savour its deliciousness, you should also practice emotional compartmentalisation to savour the fullness of life's various experiences.

Emotions and Environment

The intricate relationship between human behaviour and the environment has long been a topic of interest and debate, often framed within the context of the nature-nurture dichotomy. It is a notion widely accepted in the fields of psychology, sociology, and environmental science that the environment we inhabit can shape our actions, reactions, and even our emotional states. As someone with a professional background in Architecture and a research focus on environment-behaviour dynamics, I have delved into this subject, and the evidence is clear: the environment undeniably exerts a significant influence on human behaviour, although this influence is intricately connected with various other factors. Whether it's the classroom environment, a place of worship, a shopping mall, an office space, or a residential neighborhood, the environments we inhabit have a profound subconscious impact on our emotional states. This influence extends to the quality of the environment, affecting our thoughts, emotions, and behaviours.

Imagine a serene natural setting with abundant greenery and soothing natural sounds; such an environment often evokes feelings of calmness and tranquillity in its occupants. In contrast, a bustling and chaotic urban environment, characterised by noise, congestion, and a fast pace of life, can trigger stress, anxiety, and even feelings of unease.[3] The impact of the environment on emotional states is not limited to aesthetics alone. Factors such as lighting, temperature, air quality, and spatial layout also play pivotal roles in influencing our emotions. Research in the field of environmental psychology has consistently demonstrated how these environmental elements can shape human behaviour and well-being. In architecture and design, professionals are increasingly aware of the role they play in shaping environments that promote emotional well-being. Concepts like biophilic design, and green buildings, which integrate natural elements into built environments, are gaining prominence for their ability to enhance occupants' mental and emotional states.[4]

The environments you interact with, whether consciously or subconsciously, significantly impact your emotional states, please be conscious of this. Don't just go anywhere, be wary of where you stay and your abode. Recognising this influence is crucial for architects, designers, urban planners, and individuals alike. By understanding and harnessing this relationship, they can create environments that not only accommodate physical needs but also nurture emotional well-being. However, it's essential to acknowledge that the relationship between the environment and behaviour is not unidirectional. Your behaviour also influences and shapes the environment around you.

While training a group of mid-level managers, I once received a thought-provoking question, the participant said: *"We live in a pressured environment; how can we work without losing ourselves?"* If you work in a hostile or stressful environment. It's a situation many can relate to, and such an environment can indeed, at times, contribute to heightened negativity and hostility. However, it's crucial to recognise that, even within these challenging surroundings, you possess the ability to create your micro-climate of positivity and emotional well-being, especially within your personal space. You have the power to cultivate resilience and coping strategies that can shield you from the adverse effects of a hostile environment, at least in the short term. Furthermore, you can embark on a journey of advocacy for workplace changes, fostering a supportive and empathetic community, or even seeking out alternative environments that align better with your emotional needs. While the environment undoubtedly plays a role in shaping our emotions and behaviour, emotional intelligence empowers you to navigate even the most challenging surroundings.

In the journey of cultivating emotional self-regulation, affirmations can be powerful tools. As we close the learnings in the chapter, I want you to explore some affirmations, shared by Sohail Khan, the CEO and Founder of The Joint Venture Group. They can serve as foundational pillars for self-regulation. Are you ready for greater clarity and emotional control? Now say the following:

- I am responsible for my feelings;
- I am responsible for my behaviour;
- I always have choices about how I respond to situations, events and people;
- No one can make me upset, angry, happy, etc.
- Identifying my choices empowers me to take a fresh look at my behaviour;
- Recognising my range of choices can start changing my behaviour for the better;
- I can practice and learn new and more effective behaviours.

Highest Learning Points

Take a moment to jot down and highlight the key insights and lessons that resonated with you most in this chapter.

Most Pressing Action Points

Take a moment to note down the key decisions and actions you would take based on the insights gained from this chapter.

Chapter 4
Surmounting Hectic Traffic and Roadblocks

HOW CAN YOU EFFECTIVELY NAVIGATE through life's challenges, build resilience, and maintain a smooth emotional journey amidst the constant flow of emotions? Think about it, how? But then when we reflect on driving, what causes traffic congestion on a highway? Typically, it's the presence of a significant number of vehicles, which, in turn, slows down the overall flow and pace of movement, resulting in bumper-to-bumper traffic. Now, think about your response when you encounter a traffic jam. Do you simply abandon your vehicle by the roadside and give up on reaching your destination? Most likely not. You find ways to navigate through the congestion and continue your journey. Just as traffic congestion arises from the increased number of vehicles, your emotional highway can become jammed with the multitude of emotions you experience. However, much like you don't abandon your vehicle when stuck in traffic, you shouldn't give up on your emotional journeys.

"Dr. Abraham, I don't think you know the mixed feelings I've had recently," well, I could imagine. But I want you to own your journey; the owner's mentality is what you need now. On the emotional highway of life, emotions can sometimes create bottlenecks, impeding progress and causing a standstill. Statistics have indeed highlighted a concerning rise in cases of emotional struggles. According to statistics compiled by the Institute of Health Metrics and Evaluation, as cited by the World Health Organization (WHO), approximately 280 million individuals worldwide are affected by depression. Furthermore, more than 10% of pregnant women and new mothers experience depression. Most alarmingly, suicide claims the lives of over 700,000 individuals each year, making it the fourth leading cause of death among those aged 15 to 29.[1] In the face of these concerns, this chapter explores practical strategies and insights that can help you clear emotional roadblocks, maintain a steady and harmonious emotional flow, and build resilience to overcome life's challenges. Please come along.

The Assurance of the Destination

On the emotional journey of life, one can maintain optimism even in the face of obstacles and difficulties. This trait is commonly referred to as self-motivation, and it holds the key. When you examine high-achieving individuals within your sphere of influence, a common thread emerges: their inner drive, that unwavering determination and strength that keeps them moving forward. Do they exclusively experience positive emotions? Maybe not. However, that inner drive, that fortitude, is a more compelling force that propels you to overcome challenges and remain resolute.

So, while the road ahead may be long and fraught with challenges, you stay steadfast and patient for one prominent reason, among others: the assurance of your destination. After all, the reason you embarked on this journey in the first place was to reach a specific destination. I often humorously say that even the shortest distance has a destination. Is it true? Absolutely! Whether it's the salon, the mall, or the corner store, you had a purpose in mind before leaving your home, not to mention longer journeys and destinations. Your destination keeps you committed to the journey with the hope that you're making significant progress, regardless of the obstacles you encounter along the way. As Isaac Newton postulated in the first law of motion, "Everybody continues in its state of rest or of uniform motion in a straight line unless compelled by some external force to act otherwise." Your destination is the force that compels you to keep moving forward.

So, here's my question for you: where are you headed in life?

This is a timely and profound question. The assurance of your destination is a gift and a force that instills within you a sense of ownership as you navigate through life. You know deep down that "Nothing happens to me but for me." The mental picture of your destination is your life's vision, the very essence and purpose of your existence - the reason you were sent. That's your destination. I'm on a journey to mould minds and empower young people; that's my destination. What about you? Your destination is the highest form of motivation that propels you forward in life and along your emotional path. It transcends self-consciousness and enables you to see life and existence beyond merely living for yourself. So, this is how I put it: "It's not about me." This mindset eliminates the tendency for selfishness. Suddenly, when unhappiness loomed and I needed to write this chapter, I perceived my mission extending beyond my emotional state. Due to the urgency of my mission, my emotional state transformed. This brings to mind what Gbemisola, a participant in the Maturity, Management, and Metamorphosis Workshop (M3 Workshop), once said:

"I loved the passion of the facilitator, the clearness of terms, the relatable nature of the examples, the creativity with the visual aids. M3 Workshop was a timely wake-up call. I particularly appreciate how Dr. Abraham empathised with young adults and their exuberance without being judgemental. Sharing some parts of his own journey also made the workshop interesting and relatable. The arrangement of the modules was really thoughtful as it made it easier to connect with the new concepts. He made talking about God so interesting. Teaching is in Dr Abraham's core; he is indeed blessed with wisdom for his life's purpose. I now have a renewed sense of responsibility about what I do with my time in school, a renewed interest in organising my physical and mental space."

Have you noticed her choice of words? She described it as a "timely wake-up call." That's precisely what your life's purpose demands, and to achieve that, you need to be in the right frame of mind and emotions. However, what fuels and sustains your motivation, regardless of the emotions in play, is your destination. Despite the valuable information your emotions provide, you must also be swift and resolute about the emotional state you aspire to be in. Great achievements are unlikely with negative energy and bad emotions.

Have you seen individuals driving on the highway, seemingly lost in thought? Their hearts aren't fully present, but that shouldn't be you. Ugochi, one of my students, once shared, "With so much to offer, you always had the right thing to say at the right time, especially for me when the week had been so overwhelming, and you came into the class early in the first days of the week with a word of advice and a happy face." The key lies in the details; fellow "drivers" can perceive your level of enthusiasm. Imagine the lasting impact a "happy face" had on others. How many more people could you inspire if you had mastered your emotions?

When you look closely, we're all on an assignment; "You were sent!" The sender had a specific destination in mind for you. Much like a driver on a predetermined route, you don't choose your destination but simply follow the instructions. If you understand this, you'll grasp the next crucial insight – if God sent you, He's the best person to ask about your destination. This isn't about ambition or self-made missions; it's about the original purpose for which you were sent. Just like in highway design, if you wish to change your direction, you're free to do so by using the next available U-turn or flyover bridge. My book, "Living by Design: Go Beyond Existing to Truly Live out God's Original Design for Your Life," delves deeply into this concept, and I highly recommend it if you seek profound clarity.

However, please remember this: "It's not about you." Discovering your "Why" ignites a fresh motivation within you, enabling you to persevere through any obstacles that come your way. When I shared these principles with a group of students, one of them provided this feedback: "Dr Owoseni inspires me all the time. I could totally relate to what he taught today because my previous semester in school was one characterised by low motivation. I just couldn't bring myself to study and concentrate and I didn't even know why. I did not want the same to happen this new semester. This session has fired me up to go for more and work with my WHY. It was an extraordinary experience with Dr. Owoseni."

Redefining your Motives

In the world of work and business, it's common to engage in marketing and networking, where one of the first questions we're conditioned or expected to ask is, "What do you do?" We readily introduce ourselves with, "Hi, I'm in this profession, what do you do?" However, it's not the norm to inquire about the "why" behind someone's chosen path. Imagine flipping the script: "Hi, I'm in this profession, why do you do what you do?" It may sound unconventional, but it's a powerful question. Most people are uncertain about why they do what they do, and this lack of clarity makes them susceptible to breaking under obstacles because their motivation lacks depth. This exploration into the "why" behind our actions is what we refer to as our motives.

To get a broader understanding of this, let's take a look at intrinsic and extrinsic motivation, two major classes of motivation. Intrinsic motivation drives a person to engage in a behaviour or activity because it is inherently satisfying or enjoyable.[2] Individuals who are intrinsically motivated, pursue activities for the inherent rewards, such as a sense of accomplishment, and personal fulfillment, rather than seeking external rewards or avoiding punishment only. For example, your life purpose is an intrinsic motivation. Now you see that without a sense of your destination, you may not be driven by this motivation. When we talk about self-motivation, principally, we're talking about intrinsic motivation. This gives you high self-determination to pursue your goals and activities based on your own values and interests rather than external pressures.

If you have to wait to feel a particular way to pursue your goals, you may wait longer. Go ahead because of your selflessness and see your feelings catch up. Like Zig Ziglar said, "You don't have to be great to start, but you have to start to be great." I once heard Pastor

Bimbo Odukoya of blessed memory share a similar insight when she asked the audience. She said if you wake up in the morning, feeling bad, useless, like a failure, feeling frustrated, what do you do?" Then she revealed a thoughtful principle. She said, "If I believed everything I felt, that day would be horrible." Yes, you are aware of the feeling, but you can turn around and believe the truth: "Today is the day the Lord has made, and I will rejoice and be glad in it. Because He lives, I can face tomorrow." If you keep saying what God says, she said, soon you see your emotional state change, just because of what you believe. This is powerful! The person who committed suicide believed life wasn't fair and there was nothing more to it. Another person believed "Weeping may endure for a night, but joy comes in the morning." [3]

I could figure out that reading this book is a reflection of your intrinsic motivation, also called internal motivation. So, when you see a person engage in lifelong learning and personal development; learning a new language, taking online courses or reading books and studying without any external requirement, eventual reward or examination in view, that's a person consumed by intrinsic motivation. Similarly, intrinsic motivation often leads to higher levels of job satisfaction, personal fulfilment, and long-term commitment to tasks or activities. It's driven by a genuine interest or passion for the task itself, rather than external factors like money or recognition, as good as they are.

Extrinsic motivation on the other hand drives you to engage in a behaviour or activity solely to obtain external rewards or avoid negative consequences. Unlike intrinsic motivation, which is driven by internal factors, extrinsic motivation is rooted in external incentives or pressures like money, prizes or avoiding punishment such as criticism, or loss of privileges.[4] So you see an employee working overtime to earn a bonus or a student studying to avoid a failing grade. What about a child cleaning the room to earn a reward from their parents, or a person adhering to a diet and exercise plan to achieve a specific weight loss goal? Are those bad? Definitely, not! Both intrinsic and extrinsic motivation play a role in the journey of life and emotional intelligence. However, your internal motivation must be higher than your external! A student from my teaching audience once shared this testimonial with me after a similar session:

"I woke up this morning and the first question that popped into my mind was why I was becoming lazy and so unmotivated. I'm a first-class student and frankly, I'm intelligent but that is no longer enough for me. I'm constantly searching for something, trying to be better. I know God's purpose for my life is far more than my grades in school. Attending TMC class this morning and hearing your session on motivation especially the "asking yourself why" has sparked something in me. I'm more than grateful that I didn't miss this class, in fact, I wrote in my journal today and not in my notes. Thank you very much, sir! I pray your oil never ever runs dry and I also pray that this doesn't end with a spark, but it births real-life changes in me, God bless you richly."

Now you see how your internal motivation is your principal destination. Fundamentally, nothing else can replace that, not even an extrinsic, external motivation. Even a first class wasn't enough motivation, think about the situations around you now, "What have I based my motivation on that is now not able to sustain me?" In that feedback, the mistake the student made was making a first-class a motivation, as against being an outcome of the right motivation. The reason is this, if you base your motive only on externals, it only gives a false destination; it looks like a destination, but not a fixed destination. It can be removed without your notice. What if the bonus is not given again although it was promised, and the award and recognition don't come, what will you do? If you had based your motive just on that, suddenly hopes are dashed, that can be draining. I like to put it this way, extrinsic motivation are like the billboards and signposts on a highway; you see several of them, some digital, some overhead. They were not the reason you set out on motion, anyway. Although you get to see them in split seconds as you drive past, they make the journey interesting and road scenery visually appealing, but your destination is the ultimate drive that keeps you in motion. So, what can you do? First, be certain about your destination in life, "Where am I going exactly?" Make an action point of this if you're still unsure and unclear about it. Secondly, begin to re-align every task, and activity towards that destination.

You might have heard me share my first profound experience with extrinsic motivation. When I was in junior high, my dad promised me a BMX bicycle with one condition – to come first in class. That became my sole motive for excelling in school that term. I vividly recall how I zealously tackled assignments, paid close attention in class, and studied diligently for exams. It worked, and I clinched the top spot, earning that brand-new BMX bicycle. I was as proud of my dad for keeping his promise as he was of my achievement.

As I progressed in my educational journey, I eventually finished with a first-class degree, but now not only because of an external motivation but because of an internal one. I had grown in maturity and knew the 'Whys' of basic things in life. Intrinsic motivation now drove me more than extrinsic factors, although they still played a role. This is where I want you to arrive. When you reach this point, your emotions are under your control, and you're no longer at their mercy.

Think of it this way: a child needs external motivation to get started, but what keeps one going is internal motivation. Extrinsic motivation isn't inherently bad; you simply shouldn't rely solely on external factors. Looking at the examples I shared earlier, see how the shift towards internal or intrinsic motivation is: the employee is now driven to work extra hours not just for the bonus but because of the genuine passion for the job and the immense satisfaction from completing challenging tasks. A student now dedicates hours to studying, not solely to avoid a failing grade, but because they have a deep curiosity and love for the subject matter. They find joy in acquiring knowledge. A child eagerly cleans the room not just for a reward but because a clean room is hygienic and makes everywhere organised. Now you diligently follow your diet and exercise plan, not only to achieve your specific weight loss goal but because you value your health and well-being as essential to fulfill God's purpose. Now you see that intrinsic motivation is often more sustainable and leads to a higher level of self-determination and commitment to your goals. Your actions become purposeful and purpose-driven. Just before the COVID-19 lockdown in 2020, a student from the Youth Development Club I founded in 2014 in Nigeria reached out to me with a Facebook message:

"Hello sir, my name is Taiwo, I was once a member of the Youth Development Club at Vetland Senior Grammar School then, but now a Civil Engineering student at the Federal University of Agriculture, Abeokuta (FUNAAB). Looking back on those times when value was being added to us at the club, I never knew it would be so much instrumental in shaping me into the kind of young person I have grown to become. It was one of those things that helped me into getting my goals and I want to say thank you for your work back then. Thank you for shaping and inspiring a lot of young lives; thank you for giving back and adding value. Just as a lot of values were added to me back then, I have made it my newfound purpose to also add values to younger generations and also as an advocate for women and girls."

In hindsight, as I pondered my journey before establishing the club and initiating the weekly life skills mentoring for students, I encountered discouraging words from certain stakeholders. However, my intrinsic motivation for creating the centre far outweighed those discouragements. You can't lease it to others or let negative emotions take over. Just imagine if I had given up or turned away from setting up the centre – how many more lives I would have missed the opportunity to impact. This is the transformative power of self-motivation; you have to own it and steer your emotional states in alignment with your destination.

On Your Journey to Transcendence

As you progress through life, the pinnacle of reaching your destination is what we define as transcendence. Regrettably, not everyone attains this elevated state. But that is where God wants you to get to. Why do some individuals achieve it while others do not? The answer lies in their motivations. Different forms of motivation yield different results. If you examine Abraham Maslow's theory of human motivation, you'll notice the hierarchy of needs, with the broadest base representing the majority of the human population striving to meet basic physiological needs like food, shelter, and clothing.[5] While these are essential, if they become your sole driving force, you may lose sight of the path to transcendence.

When you work not just for monetary gain but to solve problems, express your potential, and engage in purpose-driven endeavours, you operate at a different level. This distinction influences the results you achieve and how rapidly you progress toward transcendency. Those who work solely for money can be easily disheartened by delayed pay or reduced bonuses, while those aligned with a vision diligently operate as if they own the business. The apex of Maslow's hierarchy represents self-actualization, which I refer to as purpose fulfilment, as it transcends personal desires. This is the pinnacle of exaltation and fulfilment, the state of transcendency. Self-motivation plays a crucial role in swiftly ascending and rising above the baseline on your journey to transcendency.

"And why do you worry about clothes? Look at the flowers in the field. See how they grow. They don't work or make clothes for themselves. But I tell you that even Solomon with his riches was not dressed as beautifully as one of these flowers. God clothes the grass in the field like that. The grass is living today, but tomorrow it is thrown into the fire to be burned. So you can be even more sure that God will clothe you. Don't have so little faith! Don't worry and say, 'What will we eat?' or 'What will we drink?' or 'What will we wear?' All the people who don't know God keep trying to get these things. And your Father in heaven knows that you need them. The thing you should want most is God's kingdom and doing what God wants. Then all these other things you need will be given to you.[6]

Strengthening your Motivation

Your motivation needs strength, or else it may soon wane. How do you achieve this you? Or maybe you're currently lowly motivated to life, to your work, to your family, your studies and you need strength to get back on your feet, strength has come for you. Read this testimonial from Samuel:

"I was fighting laziness, procrastination and the ability to be more international about growth in all areas of life. I was also concerned about not really having a mentor I can always reach out to as well as not having real friends and siblings that are intentional about their growth in some areas of life. Because of M3 Workshop, I have garnered the strength to be intentional about my growth, be diligent and disciplined and I will say of a truth I'm working to be a better person right now. I have also understood that perspective is everything and in a place of divinity, there is a place for restoration as God is a restorer of times and seasons and I can create my atmosphere; all I need is to be urgent about my timing. My experience with Dr. Abraham Owoseni I will say is an experience of a lifetime orchestrated by God. I love the passion and intentionality of the facilitator in teaching all the modules; every module was excellently communicated. M3 Workshop has catapulted me to a realm of impact and excellent achievement in life."

I saw a recurring theme in his feedback: intentional growth. That's the summary to strengthen motivation, you have to be intentional about your growth. Talking about growth, Professor Carol Dweck's work on mindset comes in helpful. Her research reveals how beliefs impact motivation, behaviour, and achievement. Specifically her research on the concept of a fixed mindset and growth mindset has significant implications for motivation and achievement. These two approaches have implications for the strength of your motivation. Your approach matters, the way you see things and your perspective. In the words of Lou Holtz, "It's not the load that breaks you down, it's the way you carry it."

On one hand, people with a fixed mindset believe that their abilities, intelligence, and talents are static traits that cannot be changed. They tend to avoid challenges, give up easily when faced with obstacles, and are less likely to put in effort because they fear failure. Failure, in their view, is a reflection of their inherent inadequacy. On the other hand, individuals with a growth mindset believe that their abilities can be developed and improved through effort, learning, and perseverance. They embrace challenges as opportunities for growth, see failure as a stepping stone to success, and are more likely to put in sustained effort to achieve their goals.[7] If you must be able to strengthen your motivation, then you would need the growth mindset approach to the various emotions you experience. Even when you go through difficult seasons, see it as an opportunity for growth. As Ryan Blair noted, "If it is important to you, you will find a way. If not, you'll find an excuse."

Highest Learning Points

Take a moment to jot down and highlight the key insights and lessons that resonated with you most in this chapter.

Most Pressing Action Points

Take a moment to note down the key decisions and actions you would take based on the insights gained from this chapter.

Chapter 5

Considering Other Road Users

IN THIS CHAPTER, WE EMBARK ON A JOURNEY to explore a fundamental facet of emotional intelligence: empathy. Just as a skilled driver must navigate the road while being aware of and considerate toward other road users, you, also, must traverse the delicate pathways of human interaction with a deep sense of consideration and respect for the emotions and needs of those who share your journey.

If you look closely, you can see that the last three principles we've explored—self-awareness, self-regulation, and motivation—fundamentally contribute to enhancing your intrapersonal relationships. They focus on understanding and managing your own emotions and motivations. Now, as we delve into the final two principles—empathy and social skills—we shift our focus toward improving your interpersonal relationships. These principles are designed to help you connect with and relate to others more effectively, fostering healthier and more fulfilling social interactions.

One timeless example of empathy comes from the teachings of Jesus. As he prepared to impart his wisdom, he noticed that the people gathered before him were hungry. Instead of proceeding with his lesson without a second thought, he chose to address their immediate need by providing nourishment. This act of empathy showcases a profound understanding of the emotions and physical needs of those he sought to teach.

"When Jesus received the news of John's death, he withdrew from there by boat to a deserted place, alone. When the people heard where he was headed, they followed him on foot from many towns. As Jesus came ashore, he saw the massive crowd and felt deep compassion for them, so he healed their sick.

When it began to twilight in the evening, the disciples approached Jesus and said, "This place is really remote, and it's getting quite late. So send the crowds home so they can go into the villages and buy food for themselves."

But Jesus said, "There's no need to send them away. You give them something to eat." They replied, "But all we have is five barley loaves and two fish." "Let me have them," Jesus replied. Then he had everyone sit down on the grass as he took the five loaves and two fish. After he prayed a prayer of thanksgiving over the food, he broke the bread and gave it to the disciples, and then the food was given to the people. Miraculously, the food multiplied, and everyone ate until they were satisfied. Afterwards, the disciples picked up the leftovers, and there were twelve baskets full!"[1]

Empathy: The Connecting Bridge

I have a deep appreciation for interchanges when I'm behind the wheel, whether it's navigating a ramp or a gracefully curved bridge that ushers me into a new direction. There's something truly captivating about the control I feel as I manoeuvre the steering wheel, through those captivating urban landscapes. Such a beauty of engineering; how two levels were connected to form a continuous motion. It's the same on the emotional highway. Everyone won't be at the same level of refinement, thoughts, exposure and perspective. Just like the intricacy of interchanges, people are equally complex; it's the beauty of humanity. Imagine you're in a board meeting and everyone's view is the same, won't that call for worry? But in the diversity of the views, opinions, and ideas, the meeting is energised and eventually arrives at a unanimous closing.

Empathy is that bridge that connects one another – connecting ideas, perspectives, and approaches, diverse backgrounds without talking one another down, but trying to understand their views and perspectives. Empathy isn't about diminishing someone else's viewpoint or talking them down; it's about actively seeking to comprehend their unique views and experiences. Albert Einstein once remarked, "Peace cannot be kept by force; it can only be achieved by understanding." The bridge of empathy paves the way for the peaceful coexistence of diverse thoughts and beliefs. Empathy, in essence, is the ability to step into another person's shoes, to feel what they feel, and to respond with kindness and understanding rather than judging them or accusing them. Just as Jesus demonstrated, empathy involves recognising the hunger in others, whether it be for food, companionship, support, or simply a listening ear. Talking about listening, an empathetic leader is an active listener. Most times in our human communication, we listen to respond, not to understand the other person. We listen so we can have something to say. Empathy says, listen to understand, listen more without interjection and interrupting the conversation.

Many years ago, I struggled with a limiting belief—a belief that led me astray and hindered my understanding of the world. I was firmly convinced that if I could perform a specific task in a particular way, then it should be a universal capability for everyone. It was a misguided assumption that I held onto tightly, and it took a period of quiet reflection and keen observation to identify this misconception. In hindsight, I realise that someone might have attempted to correct my perspective, but I was, perhaps, too adamant to heed their advice. It was only as my knowledge and awareness expanded, that I began to perceive the fallacy in my thinking. I came to understand that not everyone possesses the same skill set, enthusiasm, life experiences, exposure, and access to mentors as I do. My transformational journey began to take shape when I got introduced to neurolinguistic programming. This discipline unveiled the profound concept of the "map of the world."

It dawned on me that each person's perspective, their unique worldview, is likened to a map that charts their individual experiences, emotions, and beliefs. Each individual possesses their unique model of the world. To effectively communicate with someone, particularly when you aim to influence their perspective or actions, you must commence your engagement from their vantage point.[2] It's about acknowledging the diversity of these internal maps and embracing the fact that each person's journey is unique. In the words of Daniel H. Pink, "Empathy is about standing in someone else's shoes, feeling with his or her heart, seeing with his or her eyes. Not only is empathy hard to outsource and automate, but it makes the world a better place." Through empathy, we bridge the gaps between our individual maps of the world, creating connections and fostering a deeper understanding of the human experience. It is a profound tool that enriches our interactions, paving the way for a more compassionate and harmonious world.

Empathy and Active Listening

> *People don't care how much you know until they know how much you care.*
> — *Theodore Roosevelt*

In the context of our emotional journey through life, empathy is the bridge that connects you to the emotions of those you encounter. It enables you to navigate the complexities of human interaction with grace and compassion. Like a skilled driver who considers the actions and needs of fellow road users to ensure safe and harmonious travel, practising empathy allows you to coexist

111

harmoniously with those you share this emotional road with. I remember a beautiful memory when I was training a class. I noticed all the participants were tired. Rather than continue yelling out facts, gazing at my presentation slides and speaking passionately like I always do, I sensed the need to energise the audience and give a short stretch break even though it wasn't officially time for that. Empathy is the substance of our humanity. Not everything will be said verbally, you must be able to read non-verbal cues to practice empathy. Research by Dr. Albert Mehrabian suggests that communication is 7% verbal and 93% non-verbal, emphasising the importance of active listening in understanding non-verbal cues such as body language and tone of voice.[3]

Active listening and empathy are essential components of effective communication and building strong relationships. Active listening is a communication technique that involves actively focusing, understanding, interpreting, and responding to what a speaker is saying with the goal of comprehending their message accurately.[4] Active listening enhances understanding, reduces misunderstandings, fosters trust, and strengthens relationships in various contexts, including personal and professional settings. "The most basic of all human needs is the need to understand and be understood. The best way to understand people is to listen to them." Says Ralph G. Nichols.

This requires lots of intentionality and humility. As Alan Alda puts it, "Listening is being able to be changed by the other person." Empathy fosters emotional connections, promotes compassion, and supports effective conflict resolution. It's a fundamental skill in building positive relationships. Stephen R. Covey, author of the bestselling "The 7 Habits of Highly Effective People" rightly noted, "When you show deep empathy toward others, their defensive energy goes down, and positive energy replaces it. That's when you can get more creative in solving problems."

The Mirror of Humanity

Just as a vehicle relies on its windshield, side mirrors, and centre mirror for visibility, humanity requires empathy as its mirror. With these tools, you can see and understand how others are faring on the road, enabling you to adjust your actions accordingly. In the words of the renowned author Harper Lee, "You never really understand a person until you consider things from his point of view... until you climb into his skin and walk around in it." For instance, if another driver signals their intent to change lanes. You have a choice – to ignore or to allow. What's going on in the mind of that driver? Perhaps there's a need to make a turn soon. You begin to ponder their perspective, and most often, you accept their signal with a courteous slowdown or a friendly flash of your lights. This simple act on the road is a demonstration of empathy. It's about putting yourself in the shoes of others.

How about a situation where a vehicle breaks down on the fast lane? As you pass by, vehicles in the fast lane merge into your lane. You could choose to block them out of annoyance. But where is your humanity in such a reaction? It's a reflection of our choices in human relationships. The lesson here is simple - choose empathy, even when you're in a hurry. I understand you have your moments of urgency. But remember the difference between pressure and urgency: pressure is an external force, while urgency is an internal one. Don't let the reactions of other road users dictate your behaviour. Instead, choose your behaviour ahead of time. Always put yourself in the shoes of others. That's the secret to winning hearts.

Let me share a story from my teaching experience. Many years back after a session, a young man by the name, Yove approached me. He wanted further guidance and he shared with me what stood out to him from the session. According to him, it wasn't the technical jargon I'd discussed, as applicable and good as they were. It was a quote I'd mentioned by George Eliot: "It is never too late to be what you might have been." Why did this quote resonate? Because I had put myself in the shoes of my audience. I understood their needs and concerns, and I tailored my message accordingly. When I address CEOs, I pinpoint the areas that resonate with their challenges, tailoring my talk or presentation to address those specific pain and purpose points. Similarly, when mentoring young adults, my deep understanding of their perspective allows me to deliver sessions that captivate their interests and drive home key points effectively. As the American writer Maya Angelou once said, "I've learned that people will forget what you said, people will forget what you did, but people will never forget how you made them feel." Empathy is the bridge that connects you to people on a profound level. It shows that you care and breaks down all communication barriers.

For leaders in the C-Suite and business executives, don't just rattle off numbers, rankings, and spreadsheets. Remember to address how these metrics affect your team members. They're thinking, "How does this impact me?" "How does this help me?" Understand their perspective and adjust your approach. Now you know this, re-align your approach and witness the transformation in your people skills and how connected your team becomes! Don't lose them, the ball is in your court if they are connected and committed to the team's vision or otherwise; don't lose them, be a heart-centrered leader.

As one of my mentors, Mr. Tayo Olosunde will say, "Leadership is a privileged lifestyle of empathy, vision, faith, influence, and courage that places one at the peak of the pack!" Create workplaces that aren't just efficient but compassionate, where individuals aren't mere cogs in a machine but cherished contributors to a shared vision. If you find yourself in a leadership role, whether it's leading a team, managing a business, or overseeing an institution, it becomes your paramount responsibility to assess the emotional intelligence of your systems and policies. Neglecting this aspect can inadvertently hinder personal growth and development among your team members.

In business, empathy is your compass for creating people-centred products and services. How can you know what people need without empathy? Remember, empathy isn't sympathy. Sympathy ends with a pity party, while empathy takes it further, using the knowledge retrieved about potential clients and users to craft solutions that align perfectly with the market's psychographics. As Steve Jobs, the co-founder of Apple Inc., once said, "You've got to start with the customer experience and work back toward the technology – not the other way around." Empathy is the key to understanding that customer experience.

Where is your humanity if you can't put yourself in the shoes of others?

The Limitedness in Human Relations

Imagine the world as a vast, interconnected network of emotional highways, with each individual charting their course through this complex web of feelings, memories, and perceptions. As you encounter others on this journey, it becomes imperative to acknowledge that you are merely a passenger on each other's emotional roads. You might catch a glimpse of the scenery, but you can never truly fathom the entirety of someone else's inner world. You are limited in what you know about others; so, what next? Be gentle with people.

To be gentle with people is to recognise the limitations of your knowledge about them. Like fellow travelers you meet on a road trip, you only see a fraction of their lives within that split second when they drive past you or when you board the same vehicle together. You witness their actions and hear their words, but you remain unaware of the deeper concerns that shape their emotions and choices. Avoid making sweeping judgments about people based on limited information. A man once attended an event and enthusiastically greeted each member of the panel with a hearty handshake. However, when he approached one person on the panel, he was met with no outstretched hand. In response, he erupted in anger, raising his voice in frustration. When he finally took his seat, someone whispered to him that the man was blind. How bad he would have felt. In the fast-paced world we live in, taking a moment to consider the hidden realities of those around us can make all the difference in fostering compassion and understanding. As I shared earlier, empathy is likened to seeing things from someone else's perspective and respecting their unique map of the world. It involves acknowledging that every individual's emotional terrain is influenced by their personal history, cultural background, upbringing, and countless other factors. When you approach others with empathy, endeavour to understand their emotional landscape, even if you can't fully explore it.

Empathy: The Power of Asking 'WHY'

In your quest to truly embrace empathy, you must be willing to ask the essential question: "Why?" This deceptively simple word holds the power to unlock profound understanding and compassion in your interactions with others. "Why does this person feel the way they do?" "Why" is an inquiry that encourages you to go beyond surface-level observations into deeper undisclosed experiences of humans. Beyond the veil of faces, imagine the depth of emotion every individual carries. Each person carries an array of memories, experiences, hopes, and fears that shape their feelings and reactions.

To truly connect with someone, you must be willing to conclude what to do or how to communicate with them based on what you've observed.

To achieve this, listening becomes a most powerful tool. Not merely hearing words but actively seeking to understand the unspoken. Invariably, when you listen with empathy, you're not just processing information; you're absorbing feelings, acknowledging vulnerabilities, and acknowledging the human being behind the words. I was about to greet a colleague sometime back, but when I saw him and the expression on his face, I changed the preconceived thoughts I had to say and rather said what I felt was more relevant to his emotion at that moment. As Theodore Roosevelt wisely observed, "People don't care how much you know until they know how much you care." Empathy is the key that opens the door to showing others how much you care. It's like the bridge that connects hearts. Empathy gives the common ground with which you can connect with people.

I was training a school on emotional intelligence sometime back and we reached a crucial juncture—the topic of empathy. To illustrate the significance of empathy, I presented some common scenarios in which teachers could demonstrate empathetic listening and responses. One such scenario involved two students having an argument on the playground and feeling upset. I asked the teachers how they would respond to such a situation and encouraged them to reflect on their initial reactions. Without the lens of empathy, many would likely have swiftly passed judgment and concluded who was at fault. However, empathy takes a different approach—it seeks to understand. An empathetic response, as I explained during the session, could take the form of saying, "I can see that you're both upset. Let's sit down and talk about what happened so we can find a solution together."

In our fast-paced world, where information flows endlessly, and opinions are abundant, true empathy can indeed be a rare gem. It's easy to forget that you don't possess all-encompassing knowledge about everyone you encounter; you only hold a small fragment of their life's story. In light of this, it becomes imperative to approach others with gentleness and understanding. Personally, I have had my moments of judgment, particularly when I'm behind the wheel. While driving, I used to find myself forming hasty conclusions about other drivers, such as, "Why is this driver going so slowly?" or "Where is this driver rushing to?" It was only when I embraced the power of empathy that I experienced a transformative shift. I began to recognise that every driver on the road operates based on the unique urgency of their destination. We all have different priorities and timelines. This realisation served as a striking reminder that, despite our differences, we are all fellow travelers on this emotional journey called life. By adopting the perspective of "Why?" and engaging in empathetic listening, you extend a hand of understanding to those who share the road with you. You offer solace, validation, and support, contributing not only to your own emotional intelligence but also contribute to a more compassionate and empathetic society.

Emotions and Communication

Your words are the conveyors of emotions, including the tonality of the expression. Your words carry the weight of your emotions, and the tone in which you express them can make all the difference in communication. Let's do a quick demonstration: If I say these words to you: "Get out, you fool!" What emotions come over you? Irrespective of the previous emotional state you were in, you suddenly feel a new negative emotion. Is that so? Yes, you feel disrespected, betrayed, belittled, name it. On another end, if I say these words to you, "I can't thank you enough," what emotions do you feel? I can guess as well that you feel satisfied, happy, and appreciated. Now, that is the power of your words and how they convey both positive and negative emotions. Use this power to your advantage in your professional, parental, marital, and social communication.

If you're in a professional meeting for example, and tensions are running high due to a difference of opinions. At that moment, you have a choice. You can choose words and a tone that escalate the conflict, leading to a breakdown in communication and potentially damaging your working relationships. Words are that powerful, once uttered, hardly can they be retrieved or forgotten. The other option you have in that scenario is to opt for a different approach. By selecting your words carefully and delivering them with a tone of respect and understanding, you have the power to de-escalate the situation and foster a more constructive discussion. Is that simple? Yes, simple but intentional. The difference between an emotionally intelligent professional with one who is not is in intentionality. Most forms of skills and intelligence are learnt consciously and intentionally. Then, over some time and usage, they become subconscious, now a reflex because the skill is now ingrained in you. You must have observed certain people like that in your work environment, maybe few but then you wonder how they get things going, well comported and yet, well refined and cultured. They were not born with it, I can tell you, it is that intentionality.

Even when you try to convey feedback, it must be done in an emotionally intelligent way. The reason is this, you are communicating with a human who has emotions. Or better put, you are communicating with a human who has the capacity to develop emotions. Humans are not machines; machines don't have feelings, humans do. Imagine a manager addressing an employee who made a critical mistake on a project. If you're the manager, you have two options. One is that you could choose to say, "You've completely messed up this project, this is unacceptable!" Guess what? This approach immediately elicits negative emotions, making it challenging for the employee to absorb feedback constructively. On the contrary, if as the manager, you choose to say, "I see that there was an issue with the project, and I'd like us to discuss how we can rectify it together." The latter approach maintains respect and opens the door for a collaborative solution. The power is your words! Always remember the words of Maya Angelou, "I've learned that people will forget what you said, people will forget what you did, but people will never forget how you made them feel." The ability to choose your words and tone thoughtfully allows you to navigate challenging situations with grace and to foster positive connections with those around you. In your social relationships, offering constructive criticism with kindness and encouragement can strengthen friendships, while reacting impulsively with hurtful words can lead to misunderstandings and damaged relationships. Think long-term so that your words and tone can build bridges and not create divides.

It's the same principle in parenting, your choice of words and tone is not just a matter of communication; it has a profound and lasting influence on a child's development. While it may be tempting to resort to shouting and harsh language when addressing a child's misbehaviour, this approach often yields only temporary compliance, at best. In reality, it can instill fear, resentment, and emotional scars that persist long into adulthood. A more effective approach is to express expectations and consequences calmly, teaching the child about responsibility and respect. The impact of negative communication is almost irrecoverable. I had a bad experience from my high school days. The classroom buzzed with anticipation as our teacher embarked on a lesson about relationships. As teenagers, the topic might have elicited some chuckles and nervous laughter. At that moment, I couldn't help but laugh slightly. Little did I know that my innocent reaction would lead to an unforgettable incident. In response to my laughter, the teacher abruptly called me a "fool" and decided to impose punishment. The teacher's choice of words and actions effectively shut me down for the rest of that class and possibly for the entire subject. Any potential for absorbing the intended knowledge vanished in the face of the deep embarrassment and humiliation I experienced. It's a day from my high school years that I'd rather not recall. Possibly, it could have been an opportunity for constructive learning and discussion, but it turned into a missed chance. As a parent and teacher, thrive to form lasting positive memories for your children and students. It doesn't mean you are not firm; it only means you're firm and informed. When I tell my students 'No,' they appreciate it. It doesn't hurt their emotions, although it corrects their actions. Remember, every word you choose and every action you take in parenting and teaching has a lasting impact. You are shaping the future through your guidance and support. It's incumbent upon us to ensure that the memories our children and students carry forward are ones that inspire, motivate, and empower them to become compassionate, capable, and confident individuals.

You are raising the next generation; don't tarnish their future memories with your actions today. It's incumbent upon you to ensure that the memories your children and students carry forward are ones that inspire, motivate, and empower them to become compassionate, capable, and confident individuals. Parenting and teaching are not tasks to be taken lightly; they are profound callings that require intentionality. You also need to work with the head and the hand without losing the hearts of your children. When you lose the heart, it's pretty hard for holistic learning to take place. Holistic learning requires the combined domains of affective (heart), behavioural (hand) and the cognitive (head) dimensions. So, I urge you to approach this learning of working with the heart with the seriousness it deserves, for it is one of the most vital skills for success in your assignment as a parent and educator and of course every field of work.

Empathy and Communication

I recall a valuable insight shared by a participant during one of my corporate training sessions on emotional intelligence. He emphasised the importance of "raising your point and not your voice" as a professional. This observation struck a chord because it highlights the subtle distinction between effectively conveying your message and simply raising your voice. Even as a parent, it's easy to fall into the trap of raising your voice without effectively getting your point across, which are two entirely different outcomes in communication. Don't assume! Imagine a communication breakdown in the workplace during lunchtime with one of your colleagues who was wrongly accused. "Why didn't you tell me that you took the drink?" Bewildered, your colleague's response, was "Which drink?" Confusion sets, "The one that was in the fridge, of course." Your colleague vehemently denies taking it. It's only when another person enters the kitchenette and admits to taking the drink that the truth becomes apparent. Now, the accuser finds it, hesitant to apologise to your colleague for the premature accusation. This happens a lot in different contexts which reminds me of Santosh Kalwar's wise words: "Walk like the lion, talk like doves, live like elephants, and love like a small child." Emotionally intelligent individuals possess the ability to navigate within these dimensions. They understand that effective communication sometimes requires the gentle and empathetic approach of a dove, gentle in your inquiry not confrontational or accusation. Clarity wins!

Maintaining composure and clarity in interactions, both professionally and personally remains a key requirement of empathy in communication. Numerous studies have shown that raising one's voice in a conversation can trigger a defensive response in the listener. This reaction often hinders effective communication and can even lead to increased stress and tension in professional and personal relationships. On the other hand, maintaining a composed tone allows for a more receptive audience, fostering better understanding and collaboration. Raising your voice may indicate a lack of emotional regulation, whereas the ability to raise your point with empathy and understanding aligns with the principles of emotional intelligence.

Highest Learning Points

Take a moment to jot down and highlight the key insights and lessons that resonated with you most in this chapter.

Most Pressing Action Points

Take a moment to note down the key decisions and actions you would take based on the insights gained from this chapter.

Chapter 6

Lubrication and Servicing

IN THE JOURNEY OF LIFE, YOU CAN'T TRAVEL ALONE. The basis of human existence is intertwined with relationships, and navigating the emotional highway requires a deep understanding of the diverse emotions of others. Just as vehicles undergo routine maintenance to ensure their roadworthiness, your relationships also demand care and servicing. Since humans have emotions, you can't do without relating to the emotions of others, including both the positive and challenging feelings. In this chapter, we explore the art of relationship maintenance and emotional servicing, exploring how emotional intelligence can help you develop social skills, build connections with colleagues, strengthen bonds with family members, and connect with acquaintances and strangers.

Vehicle servicing for instance emphasises the importance of regular maintenance, as it is in the best interest of the vehicle to be serviced periodically to prevent potential issues. Similarly, to coexist harmoniously with others on the emotional highway, there is a need for ongoing relationship maintenance and nurturing. Just like a vehicle operates based on its roadworthiness, relationships thrive when they receive regular check-ins and care to ensure they remain healthy and functional. For example, an oil change in a car involves replacing old, worn-out oil with fresh, high-quality oil to maintain optimal engine performance. Similarly, in our relationships, we may need to address and refresh certain aspects to keep them in excellent condition.

The Art of Relational Lubrication

The lubricant that facilitates harmonious interactions on this emotional highway is what I call the "OIL" of human relations. Just as oil is used in the case of automobiles to reduce friction between engine parts, every human relationship requires this "OIL" to keep the relationship well-lubricated. To explain this concept, I've created an acrostic, where "OIL" stands for:

O — Offer value

I — Invest and nurture relationships

L — Look away from selfish interests

Let's look at each one intently:

O - Offer Value: Just as high-quality oil reduces friction within an engine, offering genuine value lubricates relationships. It's about giving selflessly, seeking to enhance the well-being of others without expecting immediate returns. This means actively seeking ways to contribute to others' well-being, whether through acts of kindness, support, or simply being there when needed. By offering value, you reduce friction and create a positive atmosphere within your relationships.

I - Invest and Nurture Relationships: Relationships, like any valuable asset, require investment and nurturing. They need your time, your care, and your attention to flourish. Neglect can lead to emotional breakdowns, just as an engine without proper maintenance can seize. Just as vehicles require regular check-ups and care to ensure longevity, relationships thrive when nurtured and invested in. It's easy to view relationships solely as transactions, but this perspective can lead to strain and dysfunction. Instead, invest time and effort in your relationships, showing genuine care and interest in the well-being of others.

L - Look Away from Selfish Interests: In the grand orchestration of human connections, it's essential to occasionally shift the spotlight away from selfish interests. Focusing solely on personal gain can corrode even the strongest of bonds. Instead, let empathy and genuine concern guide your actions. In our fast-paced world, it's common to approach relationships with personal gain in mind. However, constantly focusing on selfish interests can erode the foundation of even the most robust connections. To maintain the health of your relationships, look beyond your own needs and consider the well-being of others. Shift your perspective from transactional to empathetic, and you'll find that your relationships become more fulfilling and harmonious.

Social Skills for Servicing Relationships

In human connections, some individuals excel at forging new relationships but falter when it comes to nurturing and maintaining them. This is where the concept of servicing relationships comes into play, just like a vehicle is serviced regularly to stay in optimal condition. Just as a well-maintained vehicle ensures a smooth journey, nurturing relationships through servicing guarantees the longevity and quality of these vital human connections. So, how can you achieve this? Let's explore a set of essential social skills that can elevate the quality of your relationships and your ability to service them effectively:

Servicing Through Appreciation

> *"Feeling gratitude and not expressing it is like wrapping a present and not giving it." — William Arthur Ward*

In relationships, expressing genuine appreciation holds significant power. When you express gratitude and appreciation, you acknowledge the value and significance of the people in your life. This skill involves recognising the positive contributions, actions, or qualities of individuals. By doing so, you not only strengthen your bond but also reinforce the idea that your relationship is mutually beneficial. "Dr Abraham, I'm not that kind of person," well, you can learn it. Cultivating this skill can lead to stronger connections and an atmosphere of positivity within your relationships. It encourages individuals to continue investing in the relationship, knowing that their efforts are valued and acknowledged.

It is more than a mere social courtesy; it's a potent force that can strengthen and enrich your relationships. When expressed genuinely and thoughtfully, appreciation fosters an atmosphere of warmth, trust, and mutual respect within relationships. When you convey appreciation, you acknowledge that the people in your life have made a positive impact. It sends a powerful message that their presence and contributions matter.

Please don't think that appreciation is for big gestures or extraordinary achievements. It encompasses the everyday kindness, support, and effort that often go unnoticed. By paying attention to these smaller, yet significant, acts of goodwill, you demonstrate that you value the person for who they are and what they bring to your life. When I respond to an email reply, I always ensure I appreciate the time the recipient took to read and reply. It's in the little gestures. Guess the two powerful yet simple words that convey appreciation. "Thank you!" Universal expression of appreciation that transcends language barriers and cultural differences, when you say "thank you," you convey gratitude and respect.

However, how you say it matters. Your body and looks must

join your mouth in expressing the words, "Thank you," or else it reduces in its impact. To make it more exciting, you can creatively express your appreciation using other similar words to "Thank you." That way you stay top of mind and not generic. What about expressing your thanks by saying, "I'm so grateful," "I appreciate it," and "Please accept my deepest gratitude." Many more ways to uniquely convey your appreciation, "Thank you for being such a blessing," "I can't thank you enough," "This is much appreciated," "That's so kind of you," "Thank you for taking the time to do this," "I'm beyond grateful," "You made my day." The options are not exhaustive; you may also consider, "I'm really grateful for your help," or "Words can't describe how thankful I am," among others.

A quick caveat: beware of entitlement. It deters appreciation. An entitled mentality is characterised by the belief that others should meet your needs, desires, or expectations without the need for acknowledgement or gratitude. When someone operates from this perspective, they often take the actions of others for granted and fail to recognise their efforts. Sometimes this happens a lot within close relationships; that kindness from your friend you overlooked because you thought, "Aren't we friends?" Yes you are, but appreciation doesn't refute your friendship, it rather solidifies it. Or it could be your spouse or your team leader. When last did you express appreciation to them? As a student in the university, whenever I was preparing to go on vacation, I would prepare a thank you, paper award plaque to appreciate my parents. Once I got home, I would tuck it somewhere in my parent's bedroom; I love surprises, but who doesn't? When they eventually get to see it, I can imagine the smile that comes on their faces. Then, they call me to their room and also appreciate me in return, praying and celebrating me.

Relationships that flourish are those where appreciation is freely exchanged. Take a moment each day to reflect on the people who have positively impacted your life. Whether it's a colleague who offered assistance, a friend who provided emotional support, or a family member who showed love, express your appreciation sincerely and specifically. You can maintain a gratitude journal to help your consistency of this social skill. In a comprehensive analysis conducted in 2011, encompassing an examination of 50 studies focusing on workplace motivation, it was revealed that individuals exhibit a heightened work ethic when they perceive that their contributions were being appreciated.[1] And like Carolyn Stern noted, "Thinking of our relationships as investments allows us to understand that the more we contribute, the more secure and profitable they can be for us."

Servicing Through Apology

> *"Apologies aren't meant to change the past, they're meant to change the future."* — *Kevin Hancock*

Frictions can occur and emotions can be hurt. Every relationship encounters its fair share of conflicts and misunderstandings. What do you do at such moments? Apologising when you are wrong or when your actions unintentionally hurt someone's emotions is a crucial social skill. It demonstrates humility, accountability, and a willingness to repair any damage caused. A sincere apology can mend strained relationships and rebuild trust.

Apology helps for quick resolution of disagreements and sustenance of a positive working relationship. A well-timed apology can prevent small issues from escalating into more significant problems. And guess what? You don't have to be the cause of the misunderstanding. Most times, friction lingers because of the ego of the parties involved. The other party is waiting for the other one to apologise first. And then, the disagreement lingers.

Is there someone at your workplace or within your neighbourhood you don't greet? Do you avoid them because of malice or a grudge you're holding against them? Carrying a grudge or harbouring malice can significantly jeopardise your emotional well-being and overall quality of life. You have to let go. I understand it wasn't your fault. But you see, it's not a game of who is at fault now, it is rather, who is at rest! Holding onto such negative emotions not only weighs you down but also hinders personal growth and emotional intelligence. As Marianne Williamson rightly stated, "Unforgiveness is like drinking poison yourself and waiting for the other person to die." Harbouring resentment is self-destructive in nature. By refusing to forgive and move on, you are, in essence, inflicting harm upon yourself. "Yes, if you forgive others for the things they do wrong, then your Father in heaven will also forgive you for the things you do wrong. But if you don't forgive the wrongs of others, then your Father in heaven will not forgive the wrong things you do."[2]

Apology serves as a powerful lubricant in interpersonal

relationships, smoothing over rough edges and fostering reconciliation. It's the key that can unlock the door to healing and restoration in strained relationships. The phrase"I'm sorry" carries immense weight, capable of mending emotional rifts and rebuilding trust. But how you say it also matters. Screaming "I'm sorry" may only add to the fire rather than quenching it. It has to come with a gesture of remorse and apology. Not only that, you can also be specific about what you're sorry for. For instance, "I understand how my behaviour hurt you, I'm so sorry." That shows empathy. Sometimes, it would also require immediate action. If you are truly sorry, you can't continue to do the wrong thing. As such a change of action affirms your apology. You may also need to listen without interruption or defensiveness during a resolution. This shows respect.

Sometimes, a written apology can be more impactful, especially in situations where face-to-face communication is challenging. A heartfelt letter or message can convey sincerity. Also, in a case where the offence was public or affected a group, a public apology may be necessary to address and rectify the situation. If your professional code of conduct has a stipulated way for conflict resolution, you may also want to check that so you can abide by the standard. I know how demanding this can be, but better done than never. Drop the pride, humble yourself and mend the situation as quickly as you can before it becomes so difficult to do so. Can you pause reading now and go make amends on that friction you know you haven't resolved fully yet? You know the calls you've always ignored, the messages you've overlooked; don't wait any longer, act now, please. Letting go of grudges and mastering the art of apology can lead to healthier, more fulfilling relationships and contribute to your emotional intelligence.

Servicing through Care and Recognition

"Leadership is not about being in charge. It is about taking care of those in your charge."
- Simon Sinek

People appreciate being cared for and recognized for their unique qualities and contributions. Demonstrating care involves actively listening to their concerns, showing empathy, and offering support when needed. Recognition, on the other hand, involves acknowledging their achievements and strengths. You have to be attentive and responsive to achieve this. When individuals feel genuinely cared for and recognised, they are more likely to reciprocate with trust and loyalty.

The illusion for most leaders and executives is that caring and recognition are expensive. But it's not. It's rather in the intentionality and commitment to your people. Mary Kay Ash, founder of Mary Kay Cosmetics reiterated, "There are two things people want more than sex and money – recognition and praise." Houman S. Kaji, a Strategy and Technology Fellow at Lotus Communication shared an insightful perspective on positive reinforcement motivation. He noted "If your staff does something good, tell them. And then tell them again. And again. Keep it up. Put it in writing. Send them a memo- something they can keep. Put it in the company newsletter. Add a note to their file. Whatever, but make it widely known they did well." I agree absolutely with this; as leaders of institutions, don't wait for errors and pitfalls of team members and that's when you send queries and clarifications. Celebrate them often, those little wins you overlook. You don't have to wait till the year-end, build positive memories as a culture in your team. He reiterates further, "Let them know why you are thanking them - you made my job easier - rather than just thanking them for what they did - you came in for an extra shift. Be personal. Use 'I' and 'We', not 'management'. And say 'thank you ' in the same way as you would speak. 'I want to thank you' is so much better than 'The management wants to express its gratitude.' Praise as soon as the job is done, not a week later - do it the next day at the latest. And do it every time people do something beyond their normal brief."[3]

I once read of an executive who truly desired to celebrate his executive assistant. It was his birthday. Then he came up with the idea of asking one of his EA's profound role models to record a video to celebrate his birthday. Then, a surprise was made and as the executive assistant saw the video, he screamed in excitement with tears of joy, seeing one of his cherished role models celebrating him on behalf of his leader in a personalised birthday message. If you were the EA, how would you have felt? "On top of the world?" "Unforgettable?" "Ecstatic," what other emotions come to mind? It'd definitely have been a most memorable emotional state. There are positive emotional states we never forget; they become so timeless and indelible. Attempt to create such for others, your spouse, your children, your family members, your partners and team members. As a team leader, think of organisational initiatives you can institutionalise to recognise and show more care for your people. Research by Gallup has consistently shown that organisations with high levels of employee engagement and recognition significantly outperform those without such employee recognition initiatives. Engaged employees are more productive, innovative, and less likely to leave their jobs.[4,5] Sometimes you may not be able to know the climate of your team, possibly because they don't want to give you true feedback or they are unsure of the outcome if they do such. If you have such an organisational climate, then consider bringing in consultants to help out with this. Take the care of your people as a top priority. No matter how you may be faring on other metrics, take this or utmost concern. As Peter Drucker said, culture eats strategy for breakfast. So don't lose sight of the culture and the ambience of your institution.

Away from corporates, as an individual, your words can go a long way to express care and recognition to others. Everyone has an emotional bank account; it's a default account opened for every human. And since we all have emotions, we all have this account. How do you manage this account? Through your words, you can increase or decrease your deposit. Think about it. For instance, if you want to increase your deposit for a colleague or a mentor who is celebrating a birthday, what do you say? "HBD?" "LLNP?" "Happy Birthday?" In actual fact, those kinds of words would decrease your deposit. To increase your deposit, your words have to be more intentional and thoughtful. Yes although it's called a birth-day, a birthday is not a day. It is the entrance into a year. Here's a formula I share with my coaching clients: You begin your narrative whether it is in text or video by celebrating God's gift of life, then cite a scene/memory in the outgone year on how impactful their life has been to you and others. It has to be specific; this creates bonding and makes your message stand out from the crowd. Next, say a prayer for the new year; not necessarily wishes; your prayers serve as a seed to their new year. Conclude with an outro or a parting line/sentence. For instance, "Have a great year," not necessarily day. Take on this same mindset in every of your email correspondences, and chats; be very intentional in the words you use. If you're not chanced to reply, schedule it and come back at a time you are to give a deposit. Every single day, endeavour to deposit into other people's emotional bank accounts, is that a deal? Yes, yes? Then, I'll wait to hear from you about the impact of this book when you're done. Let's start there right? I would really appreciate it. At the close of this book, you'll see a link you can use to send this to me.

Servicing through Feedback and Suggestions

"The single biggest problem in communication is the illusion that it has taken place."
— *George Bernard Shaw*

Providing constructive feedback and suggestions can be a valuable social skill. It involves sharing your thoughts and concerns respectfully and receptively, with the intent to improve the relationship and not to hurt feelings. How can you service your relationship, especially your corporate relationships with this skill? First, understand that feedback helps identify areas that may need attention, allowing for course correction and growth. When given and received constructively, feedback can lead to positive changes that enhance the relationship's quality.

This doesn't mean you lose the essence of the message or the feedback; it only means you communicate it healthily and responsively. It could be feedback to your colleague, supervisor or even to a friend. As they say, the hallmark of true friends is true feedback. It's good to also note for the sanity of your emotions that not all your suggestions or recommendations may be adopted by a system. That wouldn't mean that they are bad, but they may not be congruent to their strategic plan or other factors that are not within your purview. Also, when communicating your feedback, don't take it personally; use professional narratives, and cite case studies of your ideas and examples. Highlight the pros and cons, then leave the decision to the management.

Here are some phrases that can help you provide feedback or

suggestions in a constructive and non-confrontational manner. Moreover, they encourage open dialogue and collaboration. Here you go: "I'll suggest...," "How about...," "Have you considered...," "I think it could be helpful to...," "It might be worth exploring...," "If I may, I'd like to propose...," "It could be beneficial to...," "Can we consider...," "What are your thoughts on...," "Perhaps we could...," "How do you feel about...," "An alternative approach could be..." and so on. Which of them do you think would be very helpful in your context?

To drive this home, here are some of the phrases used in full sentences to operationalise them:

"It could be beneficial to incorporate more visual elements into the presentation to engage the audience better."

"Can we consider streamlining our communication process to improve efficiency?"

"What are your thoughts on implementing a flexible work schedule to boost employee morale?"

"Perhaps we could explore new marketing strategies to reach a wider audience."

"It might be worth trying a different project management software to improve team collaboration."

"How do you feel about setting specific goals to measure our progress more effectively?"

"An alternative approach could be to allocate resources differently to optimize project outcomes."

"If I may, I'd like to propose that we conduct regular training sessions to enhance our team's skills."

"I think it could be helpful to brainstorm ideas for organising a team-building event to strengthen our workplace relationships."

Over to you, put them to use, and continue steadfastly. You'll naturally attract other bright minds to you because they'll love to work with you.

Servicing through Friendliness

> *"Too often we underestimate the power of a touch, a smile, a kind word, a listening ear, an honest compliment, or the smallest act of caring, all of which have the potential to turn a life around."* — *Leo Buscaglia*

Friendliness is a valuable social skill that contributes to positive interpersonal relationships and enhances your ability to connect with others. It involves being approachable, warm, and courteous in your interactions with people. Being friendly will help you to easily build rapport and grow your social capital. Networking isn't a burden for friendly people; it's your humanity. Not even a preserve of some personality type. The theory of reciprocity is a fundamental concept in social psychology, economics, and sociology. It refers to the human tendency to respond to positive actions with positive actions in return. When someone does something beneficial to you, you often feel an obligation to reciprocate, creating a sense of mutual exchange and fairness in social interactions.[6] Friendliness often triggers a sense of reciprocity, where people feel compelled to respond in a friendly manner when they encounter friendliness. This reciprocity fosters positive relationships. All you have to do is be friendly, and you can easily grow your business leads and reach potential clients.

"Dr. Abraham, I'm not a people person," "I'm shy," "That's just how I am, not too friendly." Being friendly doesn't change your personality; it only arms you with the wisdom to get the best from relationships. Approaching relationships with a friendly and approachable demeanour can set a positive tone for interactions. For instance, a smile, and your cheerful pleasantries – that does the magic. Your high energy and kind greetings without waiting for the other party to greet first. This social skill involves being warm, welcoming, and considerate in your interactions with others.

A friendly disposition encourages open communication and fosters a welcoming atmosphere. Friendliness can break down barriers, ease tension, and create an environment where individuals feel comfortable and valued. It's a continuous and foundational aspect of servicing relationships. Now that you have this new level of emotional intelligence, share the positivity with the world! Be generous with your life. "I'm putting you on a light stand. Now that I've put you there on a hilltop, on a light stand—shine! Keep open house; be generous with your lives. By opening up to others, you'll prompt people to open up with God, this generous Father in heaven."[7]

Friendliness also connotes that you're gentle with your words. A few examples, rather than say, "Be quiet!" A friendly person would say, "Can you use a softer voice?" Rather than say, "Do you have questions?" That's already a difficult answer, most likely, your respondents will say, 'No.' A friendly person will rather draw out the questions from them by saying, "What questions do you have?" Rather than say, "Are you okay?" A friendly person will use a more gentle tone and say, "How are you feeling?"

As good as being friendly is, please note that there's a difference between being friendly and who becomes your friend. Oh yes. Not the same. Yes, you're friendly. That doesn't mean that everyone is now your friend. The principle hasn't changed, "Be friends with those who are wise, and you will become wise. Choose foolish people to be your friends, and you will have trouble."[8] "Become wise by walking with the wise; hang out with fools and watch your life fall to pieces."[9]

Please be circumspect about that and be conscious to draw the line. "Don't be friends with a person who becomes angry quickly. Don't keep company with people who become angry easily. If you do, you may become like them, and then you might have trouble."[10] "...Bad temper is contagious—don't get infected."[11]

Highest Learning Points

Take a moment to jot down and highlight the key insights and lessons that resonated with you most in this chapter.

Most Pressing Action Points

Take a moment to note down the key decisions and actions you would take based on the insights gained from this chapter.

Chapter 7

Licenses and Renewals

JUST AS YOUR VEHICLE PAPERS, INCLUDING YOUR driver's license and vehicle registration, authorise you to travel on the road, a similar concept applies to your emotional journey. There are specific "licenses" or qualities you should possess to navigate your emotional highway smoothly and avoid encountering issues along the way. They are your values.

A quick word for parents: As parents, your emotional "license" extends to cover your children, especially when they are still in their formative years. This is the opportune time to consciously nurture and impart essential values to the next generation. These values may include qualities like courtesy, respect, orderliness, patience, and many others. In our youth ministry, we've developed a comprehensive life skills curriculum tailored for adolescents and young adults, emphasising the importance of equipping them with these skills. It's a critical step in ensuring they are well-prepared for the transition to adulthood and can contribute to a safe and harmonious emotional highway for everyone.

Reflecting on a recent encounter, I overheard a ten-year-old confidently exclaim in a conversation, "Do you know who I am?" This statement caught my attention and prompted me to consider the significance of instilling the right values in our young generation from an early age.

Renewal of the Mind

Merely obtaining a license isn't sufficient; it requires ongoing renewal. As I previously discussed in chapter two, you're now acquainted with the concept of self-awareness. However, there exists a higher level where you can navigate your emotions almost instinctively — the realm of the subconscious. The subconscious mind operates beyond your conscious awareness and isn't subject to your immediate control.

A question that often arises is whether emotional intelligence is an innate trait. To clarify, emotional intelligence itself isn't something you're born with. Your temperament, on the other hand, is an inherent component of your biological makeup. Here's where the connection between the two lies: while your temperament is indeed an inborn characteristic, it serves as the foundation for the development of your personality. Emotional intelligence, then, emerges as a skill that enables you to refine and enhance your personality, particularly in areas where you may have perceived weaknesses.

Remember the words of Franklin Roosevelt, "Men are not prisoners of fate; they are prisoners of their own minds." There's always a need for upgrade and renewal of the mind. The reason is this: Your mental software, which is your mindset produces the soft copy of your life's hard copies which are the tangible outcomes you experience. What then can you do? Here you go: "And do not be conformed to this world [any longer with its superficial values and customs], but be transformed and progressively changed [as you mature spiritually] by the renewing of your mind [focusing on godly values and ethical attitudes], so that you may prove [for yourselves] what the will of God is, that which is good and acceptable and perfect [in His plan and purpose for you]."[1]

During one of my sessions on character development, I approached the topic by emphasising that character essentially boils down to your "CHARACTERistics." These "CHARACTERistics" are features or qualities that are typically associated with a person, place, or thing and serve to distinguish them. When you encounter these distinctive qualities, you can readily identify them. For instance, in biology, living organisms are identified based on their "CHARACTERistics": movement, respiration, nutrition, irritability, growth, excretion, reproduction, and death.

Now, over to you, as a person, what are your own defined "CHARACTERistics"? These are your character traits and your attitudes. You may currently exhibit certain traits, but there might be some you don't particularly like, and undoubtedly, there are others you aspire to possess. How can you bring about this transformation? It starts with altering the soft copy—the core values that underpin your character. In essence, your attitude serves as an external reflection of your internal values, beliefs, and expectations.

When we discuss the traits you may not be fond of, we often refer to them as character flaws. A vital question to consider is, "Do you like yourself?" If you were to gaze at your reflection in a mirror, would you appreciate your "CHARACTERistics"? Values, in this context, encompass the standards and traits that a person consciously and unconsciously upholds.

Let me explain the concept of the soft copy-hard copy analogy. Imagine you've printed a document, say a letter, and upon inspecting the hard copy, you spot several typographical errors. What's your reaction? Do you collapse in despair, overwhelmed by the mistakes? Of course not. Instead, you return to the soft copy, rectify the errors, save the document, and then print a corrected hard copy. It's a straightforward process. Now, apply this to your values. Suppose you notice a certain attitude or characteristic in yourself that you're not fond of, and others have also hinted at it. What do you do? Just as you would with the document, you go to the root of the issue, which is your values, and make changes. I'll guide you through this shortly. In due time, people will notice a transformation in you, and they might even mention it. You'll respond with a smile and gratitude. This is the power of renewal. Change is not only possible; it's within everyone's reach, and personal growth is attainable for all.

This is an essential concept to grasp because your attitude holds the power to directly influence your emotions. For instance, if you maintain a positive attitude toward your job, it's more probable that you'll experience happiness and satisfaction when you think about or engage in your work. Conversely, harboring a negative attitude can result in emotions such as frustration or anger. Your attitude and values serve as the architects of your emotional responses in a multitude of situations and circumstances.

To illustrate, if you place a high value on honesty, encountering dishonesty in others might trigger emotions like anger or disappointment. Your attitude and values function as filters that shape your interpretation and reactions to the world, thereby influencing your emotional states. Having a robust, positive attitude and aligned values can significantly contribute to emotional resilience. For example, if perseverance is a deeply held value, you're more likely to maintain emotional resilience when faced with setbacks or challenges, sustaining a determined and optimistic outlook.

Now, you can appreciate the profound connection between your values and emotions. Your values empower you to consciously select a refined mode of response, irrespective of the circumstances, for different emotional states. For instance, you can establish new values for your attitude toward money, people, God, learning, and leadership, among other aspects of your life.

I will share an exercise for you to do shortly. But have you ever encountered the notion that someone will eventually outgrow a particular behaviour with the passage of time? What often becomes evident is that time alone doesn't facilitate change; it merely reveals the status quo. The true catalyst for change lies in how you utilise that time. There are certain traits and behaviours that, if left unaddressed, may eventually prompt others to maintain a respectful distance, all under the guise of not wanting to hurt your feelings. The sooner you take control of these aspects of your character, the better. This is where values come into play; they serve as your compass for personal growth and help you shed the behaviours you've identified as needing improvement. As William Jones observed, "The greatest discovery is that human beings, by changing the inner attitudes of their minds, can change the outer aspects of their lives."

Here is an exercise I want you to attempt, please take this very seriously. Ask yourself: currently as of today, what attitude or 'CHARACTERistics' do I exhibit and I'm not fond of? What have I been telling myself about it? Here are a couple of examples to guide you. If you truly desire a change, this is your long-awaited opportunity. Look at the examples and think about attitudes you need to also work on:

Attitude/ 'CHARACTERistics' *(What people see – the hard copy)*	Value Statement *(What you say within; self-talk – the soft copy)*	The Value *(Negative)*
Avoids taking on responsibilities, and procrastinates on important tasks. Prefers leisure and entertainment over productive work. Resists putting in extra effort or going the extra mile.	Work is a burden, and I should avoid it whenever possible. Immediate pleasure and comfort are more important than long-term success. I deserve to relax and do as little as possible.	Laziness
Demonstrates a lack of consideration for others. Ignores personal boundaries and disregards the opinions of others. Uses derogatory language.	I am superior and more important than others. My needs, opinions, and desires take precedence over anyone else's. Respecting others is a sign of weakness, and I must assert myself.	Disrespect
Engages in dishonesty, manipulation, or lying to achieve personal gain or advantage.	I can achieve my goals at any cost, even if it involves deceit, is acceptable.	Deceitfulness
Believes they deserve special treatment, privileges, or rewards without putting in the necessary effort. Always procrastinates and complains a lot.	I should receive more than others because I am inherently superior to them.	Entitlement
The feeling of inadequacy, feeling inferior to others, low self-esteem	I am not good enough; I don't feel qualified to do this. I'm shy of what people will say	Inferiority Complex

Feels envious of others' success, possessions, or achievements and may resent or undermine them.	My worth is determined by what others have, and their success diminishes my own	Jealousy

Over to you now, use this blank table and fill in your responses. You're walking free from them as you first, identify them:

Attitude/ 'CHARACTERistics' (What people see – the hard copy)	Value Statement (What I say within; my self-talk – the soft copy)	The Value (Negative)

Attitude/ 'CHARACTERistics' (What people see – the hard copy)	Value Statement (What I say within; my self-talk – the soft copy)	The Value (Negative)

Attitude/ 'CHARACTERistics' (What people see – the hard copy)	Value Statement (What I say within; my self-talk – the soft copy)	The Value (Negative)
Attitude/ 'CHARACTERistics' (What people see – the hard copy)	Value Statement (What I say within; my self-talk – the soft copy)	

What positive attitude/'CHARACTERistics' do you now desire for each of the ones you have identified? I call it, the law of replacement. Here are a couple of examples to guide you. Look at the examples and think about attitudes you need to incorporate to enjoy positive emotional states:

Attitude/ 'CHARACTERistics' *(What people see – the hard copy)*	Value Statement *(What you say within; self-talk – the soft copy)*	The Value *(Positive)*
Strives for excellence, consistently gives 100%, works diligently on tasks, thoroughly researches and puts in maximum effort.	I will put in my very best at all times and pay the price for my dreams. I will stand before kings, so I won't sit idle wasting away time. Hard work pays off	Diligence
Shows empathy and kindness to others, lends a helping hand, and seeks to understand and support people.	Making a positive impact on the well-being of others is essential, and kindness is a powerful force.	Compassion
Maintains a hopeful outlook, sees opportunities in challenges, and believes in a bright future.	Positivity and optimism lead to a fulfilling and joyful life journey. Nothing is impossible for me.	Optimism

Attitude/ 'CHARACTERistics' *(What people see – the hard copy)*	Value Statement *(What you say within; self-talk – the soft copy)*	The Value *(Positive)*
Upholds honesty and ethical principles, keeps promises, and maintains a strong moral compass.	Trust and integrity are foundational to meaningful relationships and a successful life. I won't trade compromise.	Integrity
Maintains a hopeful outlook, sees opportunities in challenges, and believes in a bright future.	Positivity and optimism lead to a fulfilling and joyful life journey. Nothing is impossible for me.	Optimism

Over to you now, use this blank table and fill in your responses (ensure each positive attitude and value counters the previous negative attitude and value you identified):

Attitude/ 'CHARACTERistics' (What people see – the hard copy)	Value Statement (What I say within; my self-talk – the soft copy)	The Value (Positive)
Attitude/ 'CHARACTERistics' (What people see – the hard copy)	Value Statement (What I say within; my self-talk – the soft copy)	

Attitude/ 'CHARACTERistics' *(What people see – the hard copy)*	Value Statement *(What I say within; my self-talk – the soft copy)*	The Value *(Positive)*

Attitude/ 'CHARACTERistics' (What people see – the hard copy)	Value Statement (What I say within; my self-talk – the soft copy)	The Value (Negative)

After one of my lifestyle harmony coaching clients completed a similar exercise that I shared with you, she had this to say: "I have been going through some emotional struggles in my relationship but never knew why I forcefully made that decision. Now I understand. I have been able to find peace in why I make certain decisions even when I don't like them. Abraham Owoseni is truly fulfilling his purpose with his unique way of conveying his message in simple, apt terms."

That's what happens when you have consciously defined your positive attitude and values – they begin to guide and direct your decisions without you even noticing.

Sustaining Positive Character

Merely establishing a new set of attitudes, or what we can refer to as 'CHARACTERistics,' along with their associated values and value statements, is only the initial step. The true challenge lies in maintaining and instilling these changes into your daily life. Have you wondered why television broadcasts are often referred to as "TV programs?" The rationale behind this term becomes apparent upon reflection. Our mindsets, much like the plots of television programs, are shaped over time. Just as watching multiple episodes of a show leaves a lasting impression on your mind, consistently practising your new attitudes and values will gradually transform your actions and behaviours.

The programs programme your mind with new beliefs. Just like television programs, your mindset is formed through repeated exposure and reinforcement. Therefore, sustaining your positive attitudes and values will require consistent effort. It's not a one-time event but an ongoing journey. Continuously remind yourself of the new attitudes and values; repeat your new value statements and affirmations regularly just as TV programs repeat episodes to ensure viewers remember the content.

Also, begin to act in alignment with your chosen values, even when it's challenging. It may look strange at first, but put through consistent practice, you get to solidify the changes. If you can, it is advisable to be accountable. Share your new set of values and value statements with your spouse or colleague. After a while, say one month to three, ask if they can see any of the 'CHARACTERistics' of your new attitude in your actions over the period of evaluation. Ensure you also have an environment that supports your new attitude and values. Surround yourself with people, books, and resources that reinforce the changes you want to make.

Highest Learning Points

Take a moment to jot down and highlight the key insights and lessons that resonated with you most in this chapter.

Most Pressing Action Points

Take a moment to note down the key decisions and actions you would take based on the insights gained from this chapter.

Afterword

It's been truly wonderful spending time through the book, "E-motions: How to Work with the Head and the Hand without Losing the Heart," and I'm eager to hear about your experience. Throughout this journey, we've explored notable psychological and physiological dimensions of emotions, which have provided valuable insights. However, this exploration would be incomplete without showing you a dimension that transcends all others and I'm excited to explore this profound aspect with you.

Your creator, God, is fully aware that you are an emotional being. He crafted you with intricate emotions when He made you. "Know that the LORD, He is God; It is He who has made us, and not we ourselves; We are His people and the sheep of His pasture."[1]

However, He didn't create you solely as an emotional being. Fundamentally, He designed you as a spiritual being. As humans, we exist in three dimensions: as a spirit being with a soul, residing in a physical body. God is interested in the entirety of your being, ensuring that you are whole and healthy in your spirit, soul, and body. These dimensions work together in harmony, like a linear equation: spirit to soul to body. The body receives signals from the soul while the soul receives from the spirit. "Now, may the God of peace and harmony set you apart, making you completely holy. And may your entire being—spirit, soul, and body—be kept completely flawless in the appearing of our Lord Jesus, the Anointed One."[2] "May your whole self—spirit, soul, and body—be kept healthy and without fault when our Lord Jesus Christ comes."[3] Through your spirit, you discover God's purpose, the essence of your being and remain connected to the source; through your soul, you give expression (thoughts, emotions & will) to the fulfillment of purpose on earth. Through your body, you execute and live with a sense of mission within the span of time.

When you examine it closely, you'll come to understand that your spirit is the most intricate dimension because it truly defines who you are. Then God said, "Let us make human beings in our image, to be like us."[4] What then is God's image? "God is a Spirit (a spiritual Being) and those who worship Him must worship Him in spirit and in truth (reality)."[5] You are more than your physical appearance, your demographic identity, or your external characteristics, like your height, weight or colour. "But God told Samuel, 'Looks aren't everything. Don't be impressed with his looks and stature. I've already eliminated him. God judges persons differently than humans do. Men and women look at the face; God looks into the heart.'"[6]

Furthermore, the strength of your spirit directly influences the strength of your soul. "A person's spirit can give him strength. But when someone is sick in his spirit, who can make him well again?"[7] Now you see that the weakness in your soul isn't just about the soul, it is the weakness of the spirit. If all you do ends in the realm of the soul, you may still be missing the major influence over your soul, it's your spirit. "Your inner life—the way you feel—determines your strength. Your inner life instructs you on how to respond to life's surprises."[8] So, first things first, the instruction is clear, "So above all, guard the affections of your heart, for they affect all that you are. Pay attention to the welfare of your innermost being, for from there flows the wellspring of life."[9]

As you live through life, have this picture in mind; You might have heard me share this illustration in my training and speaking engagements. Imagine this scenario: After God created you, you were in heaven, praising and worshiping Him. Then, when the time came, God looked at you and reminded you of the reason He created you in the first place. He sent you to Earth for a principal assignment. In the earthly realm, "spirits" need a vessel, a suitcase, and that is your body – the biological and physiological part of you. But that's not all; there's a "middleman," the soul, the realm of psychology and sociology. The soul connects your spirit and your body. If your spirit is the operating system, your soul is the software that makes the hardware useful. Although the body is the hardware, it still requires software to function effectively. Hence, you have a thinking mind, a decisive will, and a multitude of emotions – these make up your soul.

However, there is an attack on your soul. "Be alert and of sober mind. Your enemy the devil prowls around like a roaring lion looking for someone to devour."[10] This attack is evident in the rising cases of stress, burnout, anxiety, depression, emotional disconnection, loneliness, and the search for meaning and feelings of isolation. You might have asked yourself, "Why am I experiencing these prolonged emotions?" The answer is not elusive – there's an attack. "Why, my soul, are you downcast? Why so disturbed within me? Put your hope in God, for I will yet praise him, my Savior and my God."[11] So, maintain this awareness as you journey through life, regardless of the myriad emotions you experience. When it's all said and done, God, your creator, expects your return—the real you, your spirit. Don't let any negative emotion stop you; leverage on positive emotions as you continue to fulfill your assignment. Look to the example of Paul, who, despite facing emotional traumas, fulfilled his assignment and declared, "I have fought the good fight for what was destined for me to finish. I have kept the faith."[12]

Your soul is under attack not because of any wrongdoing or because of your past life, even if you've had a rough past life, but primarily because someone is out to steal your joy, affect your mood, thinking, and behaviour and hinder you from fulfilling God's purpose. Even the devil has a purpose, "The thief's purpose is to steal and kill and destroy. My purpose is to give them a rich and satisfying life."[13] You need to be in the best frame of mind to fulfill God's assignment for you. So, God came, "I came so they can have real and eternal life, more and better life than they ever dreamed of."[14] "I came to give life—life that is full and good."[15]. Do you want this kind of life?

Perhaps you have some degree of joy, but it's not yet complete. Some aspects of your life may still lack joy—your marriage, your career, your longing for godly children, or a fulfilling vocation. The wait may seem long, but you can have it all. I'll recommend you get my wife's book, titled, "The Wait is Over." You don't have to sacrifice one aspect for another. God's desire is clear: "These things I have spoken to you so that My joy may be in you, and that your joy may be made full."[16]

So, we have cases of depressed minds – always feeling sad, hopeless or having thoughts of suicide; some are experiencing insomnia, not able to fall asleep and enjoy good sleep. For some others, it's bipolar disorder- excessive mood swing. Maybe yours is just some form of anxiety –you're always worried and sometimes experience panic attacks or you experience attention-deficit hyperactivity disorder. Some are now addicted to illegal drugs and alcohol, looking for a way out finally. For some, it's a post-traumatic stress disorder from past traumatic events and you haven't healed from it. I'm glad to let you know that your healing has come. I know those nights of crying your eyes out, you'd tried to paint an external facade that all was going well, but deep down, you know that is not the case.

Can God really help me? Yes, He can, and He will, if you give Him a chance to, no matter how worse it appears. "God becomes angry, but he will not stay angry forever. He takes pleasure in showing his love. We may cry for the night, but when morning comes, we will celebrate."[17] In the words of Pastor Judah Ola, "Depression is not an emotion, it is a spirit. Suicidal thought is not an emotion, it's a spirit. The Bible calls it, the spirit of heaviness. That is what brings emotional assaults." You make the job of the enemy easy if you succumb to depression, suicidal thoughts, and every persistent negative emotion. Because his purpose is to steal, kill and destroy. Don't try to justify those recurring emotions with good excuses. It appears normal to you, but the adversary has a contrary plan. "You may use science to cut the branches, but the root remains a spiritual one," he noted.

What can you do now? Let's get to the roots! There are persons who can't think depressive thoughts not because everything is all rosy or that they do not face challenges, but their emotion is guarded from such spirit of heaviness. I recall a person once told me, he said, "I feel like I'm slowly losing my mind, and even the people closest to me don't care." God cares, and all He wants is for you to cast your care on Him. "Casting the whole of your care [all your anxieties, all your worries, all your concerns, once and for all] on Him, for He cares for you affectionately and cares about you watchfully."[18] Sometimes you don't even understand yourself and why you do what you do. This has denied you of building quality relationships and maintaining them. Sometimes, people find you 'strange,' and you just don't know how this happens. I can relate with you, perfectly. I hear you say this as well, "I don't really understand myself, for I want to do what is right, but I don't do it.

Instead, I do what I hate."[19] I'm sure you know the reason now. "What I don't understand about myself is that I decide one way, but then I act another, doing things I absolutely despise."[20] Your willpower alone cannot help; your spirit plays a crucial role. As I mentioned earlier, the three dimensions of your being work together in harmony, like a straight-line equation: spirit to soul to body. So, your spirit instructs, strengthens and sustains the decisions for your soul to process and eventually your body acts on.

If it feels like nobody understands your emotions and what you've been through, remember that Jesus does. He knows how you feel and all the predominant emotions that have stolen your peace, robbed your joy, and hindered your productivity. Jesus desires your happiness. You are not alone in your struggles, "Jesus understands every weakness of ours, because he was tempted in every way that we are. But he did not sin!"[21] Jesus also wept, "He was despised and rejected— a man of sorrows, acquainted with deepest grief. We turned our backs on him and looked the other way. He was despised, and we did not care."[22] This is what He says to you, "Come to Me, all you who labor and are heavy-laden and overburdened, and I will cause you to rest. [I will ease and relieve and refresh your souls.]"[23] Don't carry all those age-long emotional baggage all alone, come and lay them at His feet. Is your heart shattered and you feel it's irrecoverable? He says, come! "He heals the wounds of every shattered heart."[24] That's exactly what God wants to do for you, "He heals the brokenhearted and binds up their wounds [curing their pains and their sorrows]."[25] Your healing is already here. You might be shedding tears as you read this, longing for help. I'm delighted to announce that help has arrived. God hasn't brought you this far to leave you alone. He says, "Don't be afraid, for I am with you. Don't be discouraged, for I am your God. I will strengthen you and help you. I will hold you up with my victorious right hand."[26] Not everyone is grappling with the negative emotions that have engulfed our world today. Not all executives lack peace of mind, not all professionals are burnt out, and not everyone is perpetually frustrated. There is a way out.

You might have heard Mickey Guyton's song, "Hold On," or seen it in the movie "Breakthrough." Pay close attention to the chorus:

> So hold on, hold on
>
> Don't let go
>
> Hold on, hold on
>
> I'll be your hope
>
> I'll be your lifeline
>
> I'll never stop fighting
>
> So hold on, hold on
>
> Hold on to me, Hold on to me.[27]

One of the verses in the song says, "When you're in the dark, I'll come and find you." Your journey through this book is God's way of finding you. Would you open the door of your heart to Him? Another verse of the songs says, "If there's a prayer, I'm gonna pray it; When there's an answer, I'll be right here waiting." Indeed, there's a prayer you can pray now, and I'll be honoured to lead you in it. Say this prayer;

"Dear Heavenly Father, I come before You, recognising my need for You. I acknowledge that Jesus is the way, the truth, and the life. I confess my sins and ask for forgiveness. I invite Jesus into my heart and life, surrendering to His lordship. Thank You for Your love, grace, and the gift of salvation. In Jesus' name, I pray. Amen."

I want to congratulate you because the Spirit of God is now directing the course of your soul, and your entire being. You're not on your own. This is now your testimony, confess this along with me:

"The Spirit of the Lord, the Eternal, is on me. The Lord has appointed me for a special purpose. He has anointed me to bring good news to the poor. He has sent me to repair broken hearts, And to declare to those who are held captive and bound in prison, "Be free from your imprisonment!" He has sent me to announce the year of jubilee, the season of the Eternal's favour: for our enemies, it will be a day of God's wrath; For those who mourn it will be a time of comfort. As for those who grieve over Zion, God has sent me to give them a beautiful crown in exchange for ashes, To anoint them with gladness instead of sorrow, to wrap them in victory, joy, and praise instead of depression and sadness. People will call them magnificent, like great towering trees standing for what is right. They stand to the glory of the Eternal who planted them."[28]

If you look closely, you see that every prolonged negative emotion is a spirit and has to be replaced. For instance, heaviness is a spirit and is now replaced with the garment of praise. "To appoint unto them that mourn in Zion, to give unto them beauty for ashes, the oil of joy for mourning, the garment of praise for the spirit of heaviness, that they might be called trees of righteousness, the planting of the Lord, that He might be glorified."[29] What this means for you is that, now that you have God's Spirit living in you, He is in charge of your emotions. The Holy Spirit in you makes you happy, comforts you, gives you peace. "But the Spirit causes us to love. He also makes us happy and gives us peace. He causes us to be patient, and he is kind. He causes us to do good things. He helps us to believe and to be gentle and he helps us to control ourselves. There is no law against these things."[30]

Your New Guard: Perfect Peace and Wholeness

There is something about the peace of God; it keeps you at rest. That is the reality of those whose souls are led by the Spirit. Irrespective of the concerns, you just find out that you're at rest. It's a guard, it prevents your heart from being broken and depressed. "Don't worry about anything, but pray and ask God for everything you need, always giving thanks for what you have. And because you belong to Christ Jesus, God's peace will stand guard over all your thoughts and feelings. His peace can do this far better than our human minds."[31] Carrying weights and pains? And they're weighing you down? Jesus can help you. Self-help isn't enough. The 1855 hymn "What a Friend We Have in Jesus" by Joseph M. Scriven is evergreen. The chorus says, "O what peace we often forfeit, O what needless pain we bear, All because we do not carry, Everything to

God in prayer!" Why carry it alone? Take it all to God. Why? "Jesus knows our every weakness, Take it to the Lord in prayer." Furthermore, Scriven's hymn read, "Are we weak and heavy-laden, Cumbered with a load of care? Precious Savior, still our refuge— Take it to the Lord in prayer; Do thy friends despise, forsake thee? Take it to the Lord in prayer; In His arms He'll take and shield thee," [32]

If you now have Christ in you, then you have access to this dimension of peace. This kind of peace is not built on things or dependent on people, it stands alone on the rock that never fails, Jesus. "I have told you these things, so that in Me you may have [perfect] peace and confidence. In the world you have tribulation and trials and distress and frustration; but be of good cheer [take courage; be confident, certain, undaunted]! For I have overcome the world. [I have deprived it of power to harm you and have conquered it for you.]"[33]

In conclusion, remember this parting gift from God: "I'm leaving you well and whole. That's my parting gift to you. Peace. I don't leave you the way you're used to being left—feeling abandoned, bereft. So don't be upset. Don't be distraught."[34] This is your gift Keep it close and cherish it, even in the face of life's challenges "I am leaving you with a gift—peace of mind and heart. And the peace I give is a gift the world cannot give. So don't be troubled or afraid."[35] Now, keep and cherish that new reality, your parting gift. Don't let it be stolen by the cares of the world. Let's pray together: "Father in the name of Jesus, I declare that every concern, worry, and trouble over your heart and mind bows right now to the perfect peace of God, Amen." I see everything coming together for you. "Don't fret or worry. Instead of worrying, pray. Let petitions and praises shape your worries into prayers, letting God know your concerns. Before you know it, a sense of God's wholeness, everything coming together for good, will come and settle you down. It's wonderful what happens when Christ displaces worry at the centre of your life."[36]

Make prayers your steering wheel, not a spare wheel at times of emergencies. If you're feeling overwhelmed, pray about it and ask the Holy Spirit to help you and strengthen you. I do this a lot, "Lord, I receive fresh strength as I start this task. "This is your advantage. "Don't be pulled in different directions or worried about a thing. Be saturated in prayer throughout each day, offering your faith-filled requests before God with overflowing gratitude. Tell him every detail of your life, and then God's wonderful peace that transcends human understanding will make the answers known to you through Jesus Christ."[37]

This is your gift, your new reality. Don't let it be stolen by the cares of the world. Cherish it, and remember that God is with you, guiding your soul to a place of perfect peace and wholeness.

Highest Learning Points

Take a moment to jot down and highlight the key insights and lessons that resonated with you most from the Afterword.

Most Pressing Action Points

Take a moment to note down the key decisions and actions you would take based on the insights gained from the Afterword.

END NOTES

Chapter 1: Emotion is in Motion And I'm the Driver

[1] Kuppens, P., Allen, N. B., & Sheeber, L. B. (2010). Emotional inertia and psychological maladjustment. *Psychological science, 21(7)*, 984–991

[2] Butler, J. (2023). LinkedIn post on Emotions. Retrieved from LinkedIn.

[2] Fredrickson, B. L., & Losada, M. F. (2005). Positive affect and the complex dynamics of human flourishing. *American Psychologist*, 60(7), 678-686.

Chapter 2: Why I Drive the Way I Do

[1] Sutton A. (2016). Measuring the Effects of Self-Awareness: Construction of the Self-Awareness Outcomes Questionnaire. *Europe's journal of psychology*, 12(4), 645–658.

[3] Ekman, P. (1999). Basic Emotions. In T. Dalgleish & M. J. Power (Eds.), Handbook of Cognition and Emotion (pp. 45-60). John Wiley & Sons.

[4] Ekman, P., & Cordaro, D. (2011). What is meant by calling emotions basic. Emotion Review, 3(4), 364-370.

[5] Job 3:25 NKJV

Chapter 3: Driving with Functional Brakes

[1] Gross, J. J. (2002). Emotion regulation: Affective, cognitive, and social consequences. *Psychophysiology, 39(3)*, 281-291.

[2] David, S. (2016). Emotional Agility: Get Unstuck, Embrace Change, and Thrive in Work and Life. Penguin.

[3] Kaplan, S., & Kaplan, R. (1989). The Experience of Nature: A Psychological Perspective. Cambridge University Press.

[4] Joye, Y., & Van Den Berg, A. E. (2011). Is Love for Green in Our Genes? A Critical Analysis of Evolutionary Assumptions in Restorative Environments Research. Urban Forestry & Urban Greening, 10(4), 261–268.

Chapter 4: Surmounting Hectic Traffic and Roadblocks

[1] World Health Organization, WHO (2023). Depressive disorder (depression). Retrieved from WHO.

[2] Deci, E. L., & Ryan, R. M. (1985). Intrinsic motivation and self-determination in human behavior. Plenum.

[3] Psalm 30:5 AMPC

[4] Pink, D. H. (2009). Drive: The surprising truth about what motivates us. Penguin.

[5] Maslow, A. H. (1943). A theory of human motivation. *Psychological Review, 50(4),* 370-396.

[6] Matthew 6: 28-33 MSG

[7] Dweck, C. S. (2006). Mindset: The New Psychology of Success. New York Random House Publishing Group.

Chapter 5: Considering Other Road Users

[1] Matthew 14:13-21 TPT

[2] NLP Podcast. (n.d.). NLP Presuppositions: #6 Respect for the Other Person's Model of the World. NLP Podcast.

[3] Mehrabian, A. (1971). Silent Messages: Implicit Communication of Emotions and Attitudes. Wadsworth Publishing.

[4] Houston, P. (2019). Active Listening Skills.

Chapter 6: Lubrication and Servicing

[1] Dahl Melissa (2016). How to Motivate Your Employees: Give Them Compliments and Pizza. Retrieved from The CUT

[2] Matthew 6:14-15 ICB

[3] Houman S. Kaji (2019). Managing Your Team, Use positive reinforcement motivation. Retrieved from LinkedIn

[4] Dan Witters and Sangeeta Agrawal (2015). Well-Being Enhances Benefits of Employee Engagement. Retrieved from Gallup

[5] Gallup (n.d.) What Is Employee Engagement and How Do You Improve It? Retrieved from Gallup

[6] Robert B. Cialdini (2006). Influence: The Psychology of Persuasion. Harper Business

7 Matthew 5:15-16 MSG
8 Proverbs 13:20 EASY
9 Proverbs 13:20 MSG
10 Proverbs 22:24-25 EASY
11 Proverbs 22:24-25 MSG

Chapter 7: Licenses and Renewals

1 Romans 12:2 AMP

Afterword

1 Psalm 100:3 NKJV
2 1 Thessalonians 5:23 TPT
3 1 Thessalonians 5:23 ICB
4 Genesis 1:26 NLT
5 John 4:24 AMPC
6 1 Samuel 16:7 MSG
7 Proverbs 18:14 ERV
8 Proverbs 18:14 TPT
9 Proverbs 4:23 TPT
10 1 Peter 5:8 NIV
11 Psalm 42:11 NIV
12 2 Timothy 4:7 TPT
13 John 10:10 NLT
14 John 10:10 MSG
15 John 10:10 ICB
16 John 15:11 NASB
17 Psalm 30:5 ICB
18 1 Peter 5:7 AMPC
19 Romans 7:15 NLT
20 Romans 7:15 ICB
21 Hebrews 4:15 CEV
22 Isaiah 53:3 NLT
23 Matthew 11:28 AMPC
24 Psalms 147:3 TPT
25 Psalms 147:3 AMPC
26 Isaiah 41:10 NLT
27 Mickey Guyton (2019). Hold on. Breakthrough (Music From & Inspired By The Motion Picture)
28 Isaiah 61:1-3 TPT
29 Isaiah 61:3 KJV
30 Galatians 5:22-23 EASY
31 Philippians 4:6-7 EASY
32 Scriven, J. M. (1855). Hymn: What a Friend We Have in Jesus.
33 John 16:33 AMPC
34 John 14:27 MSG
35 John 14:27 NLT
36 Philippians 4:6-7 MSG
37 Philippians 4:6-7 TPT

THANKS FOR READING!

If you enjoyed the book, please consider leaving a compelling review on Amazon.

Your insights are not only beneficial for potential readers but also vital in our ongoing efforts to enhance our work. Thank you for taking the time to share your thoughts!

AS A BONUS,

access your free transformational guide

at www.abrahamowoseni.com

SHARE WITH ME

If you want to reach me directly and share more with me about your experience reading through E-Motions: How to Work with the Head and the Hand without Losing the Heart, please use this link https://abrahamowoseni.com/feedback

I can't wait to hear from you.
Keep building a better world through the harmony of the head, the hand, and the heart!

TRANSFORMED LIVES

"Mr. Abraham is one of the most passionate speakers I have ever met; His passion for youth empowerment is exceptional. He is the pure example of the kind of leaders and change-makers the world needs. Daniel I.O.

I love the practicality of the session. It made the class more interactive. It opened my eyes that I am not a Leader by accident that God had already prepared (from the various tasks we have handled that we feel that is irrelevant) us before we were called to lead. And for us to function well as a leader we really need to identify and attend to the needs of those that are under our care. Maduabuchi G., Convener, School on the Rock

I've gone back to the drawing board, to look at what ingredients my leadership style was lacking and also fine-tuned it to what works for me. I've been able to also understand the ripple effects my mental composure has on the people and the start-up I'm leading. I loved the aspect that talked about finding your field and playing in that field. Dr. Abraham Owoseni is a great and impactful teacher.
Derin O.

You've really got me thinking about being a whole lot clearer and intentional about what I do. I love the presentations where you feel like they were written/delivered just for you.
Sandy W., Manager, Blessed Children's Hope Foundation, Australia

Abraham Owoseni is a practical, clear, and straightforward trainer. You will always leave sessions with him with easily applied lessons that will surely help you achieve your goals and become a better person. Omoniyi T.M., National Coordinator, Threshing House

Dr. Abraham is a blessing. Since meeting him, I've had a new dimension of thought like never before. I love the way he speaks with simplicity, breaks it down to the barest level of understanding and genuinely cares that people are impacted. He is the definition of leadership.
Kingsley C., Founder, Leaders Fort Company

Abraham Owoseni was a facilitator at our 2017 in-house course and he was able to provide relevant experience and information around youth development. His expertise is unwavering and his depth in youth mentoring is incomparable.
Olumide F., CEO, Agile P3

Many things stood out for me, first, the introduction, watered my appetite and got me and other leaders fired up. I loved the perspective given to the topic; it was encapsulating, from start to finish, particularly the relatable analogies and life experiences and the structure. I gained a perspective to balance between mere survival and my journey to global relevance with a better understanding of the skills needed. Abraham Owoseni gave a perfect first impression, the warm acceptability and an unrestrained display of energy! I'm overwhelmed. I've never seen it in that fashion. Thank you, sir.

Tolulope S.

The spirit of delivery of speech by the guest, Dr. Abraham Owoseni, is highly invigorating and enthusiastic with passion, speaking with authority and conviction and reaching deep into the innermost thought of understanding of all wise trained educators. All I learned from the beginning of his speech until now is worth applauding, listening to, and applying in real life. Thank you so much, Sir.

Shogbein O.A.

"Inspirational" is always the word, I think Dr. Abraham's ability to see things through other people's lens makes his answers just on point and accurate and inspiring. Many instances mentioned were very relatable and in all very insightful! I'm now working on strategic answers prepared beforehand for vital common questions as taught during the presentation. I've also had to rethink of the reason why I'm doing what I'm doing to put it in the right perspective.

Demilade

I actually meant to send this a while ago. I attended the Revolution Summit you facilitated in July, 2022. It was a deeply insightful experience for me. It changed my perspective on the meaning of success. I understood that true success would require balance across all areas of life and would ultimately result in the growth of a person. Discovery leads to revolution and revolution must lead to evolution. I also read the Maturity Handbook. I am quite confident that with the concepts you discussed at that event, and the many more I uncover while perpetually learning through life, I am on track to lead a life of good balance. I am grateful to you and your team for putting these together for us and I have no doubts that great rewards are in line for you. God bless you richly Sir. Cheers. Isaac I.

Read more at https://abrahamowoseni.com/testimonials/

USEFUL RESOURCES

What an incredible journey it has been! I hope you found this experience valuable. Here are some other recommended books and transformational learning resources by Dr. Abraham Owoseni

Explore and Order Other Books by Dr. Abraham Owoseni:

[Category] Clarity, Career and Leadership

Lead-a-Ship: Navigating Success in Managerial Positions

Living by Design: Go Beyond Existing to Truly Live out God's Original Design for Your Life

The Next Chapter: How to Navigate the Next Season of Life With Clarity and Confidence

The Career Leader: A Guide to Purposeful Career and Influential Leadership

[Category] Relationships and Lifestyle

The Wait is Over: How Mums and Dads can Trust God to Receive their Godly Seeds by Sarah O. Owoseni

Starting a New Home: A Young Adult's Guide to a Well-balanced Family Life

Values of a Father: Fatherhood-Parenting and Nation Building

Fellows-in-a-Ship: How to Start the Friendship that Leads to Courtship Without Shipwreck

The In-Betweens: How to Navigate Relationships Beyond the Ecstasy of Rings, Flowers and Perfect Pictures

The Maturity Handbook: 30 Days of Deep Reflections, Uncommon Wisdom, and All-round Development

The Architecture of Goals: How to Design, Develop and Live Out Your Goals Seamlessly

Goal Setting Quickie: A Quick Fix to Getting Better Results & Setting Higher-Order Goals

[Category] Academics and Personal Development

Camp Us: A Memoir for a Smooth Academic Sail in the Higher Institution

Life During & After School: How to Make Schooling Fun & Exciting Without Painful Memories & Future Regrets

Explore and order at www.abrahamowoseni.com

Explore Dr. Abraham's Online Courses on Lifestyle Harmony and Development:

Self-Management Strategies: The Unconventional Lifestyle of Effective Leaders

People Skills: How to Choose Friends and Grow your Social Circle on your Terms

Workplace Success Kit: Core Skills to Turbocharge your Attitude, Charisma, and Lifestyle in the Workplace

Emotional Healing: Heal from Pain, Grief, and Heartbreaks Without Remaining Broken

The Habit Champion: How to Stop Any Unwanted Habit and Sustain Productive Ones

Confidence Upgrade: Turbo-charge your Self-worth and Regain your Self-Esteem

Explore and Enroll at **school.abrahamowoseni.com**

ACKNOWLEDGEMENTS

I'm deeply thankful for the divine grace and inspiration that guided me throughout this project. Thank you, Holy Spirit. Celebrating the pioneering work of Daniel Goleman in his 1995 book "Emotional Intelligence: Why It Can Matter More Than IQ" and the five components he shared with the world. Goleman's groundbreaking insights laid the foundation for my journey into the realm of emotional intelligence.

I extend my heartfelt gratitude to Mr. Kingsley Okere, CEO of Kemslis Pragmatic Limited, a human resource and business management enterprise, for the partnership at the emotional intelligence training sessions I facilitated with your clientele. Your support and collaboration have been invaluable.

To my past and future coaching clients, I want to express my sincere appreciation for your trust and confidence in me as your life coach. Your journeys and aspirations have enriched my own understanding of emotional intelligence, and I'm honoured to have been a part of your path to personal growth.

I am also deeply grateful to the countless individuals, mentors, and peers whose wisdom, guidance, and encouragement have contributed to the development of this work. Your collective influence has been immeasurable.

A special shout-out to the esteemed thought leaders, business leaders, and executives who graciously endorsed this book. Thank you for your investment in working and leading with emotional intelligence. I express my gratitude to Dr. Niyi Borire for the invaluable contribution to this book, particularly in crafting the foreword, is sincerely appreciated. Thank you for your inspiring work in neuroleadership and neuroscience research.

I want to extend my thanks to my family, friends, and loved ones for their unwavering support throughout this kingdom assignment. Your patience and understanding have been a veritable support system on this journey.

Lastly, I extend my heartfelt appreciation to my exceptional design and editorial team for their outstanding work and to everyone who has been a part of this journey.

ABOUT THE AUTHOR

Abraham O. Owoseni, Ph.D.

Dr. Abraham Owoseni is a versatile transformational leader on a life mission to mould minds and raise young people. With a track record of inspiring thousands to achieve their personal & corporate goals, he excels as an award-winning educator, life coach, leadership consultant, author, youth minister, global speaker, and corporate trainer.

As a recognised thought leader in the domains of education and youth development, Dr. Abraham brings a wealth of multidisciplinary expertise encompassing areas such as training and development, life coaching, publishing, youth ministry, architecture, and higher education.

Dr. Abraham has dedicated his life to the holistic growth of young people, instilling essential life skills and empowering thousands across the globe. His message of holistic development and life-skills-based teachings continues to transform several lives around the world. His journey is driven by a passion for human development and holistic growth, he focuses on improving the developmental outcomes of youth through education, environments, and empowerment.

In 2013, Dr. Abraham founded Young Breeds, a global youth ministry dedicated to raising a new breed of purpose-driven and holistically developed individuals. Through a network of Youth Development Centres, Young Breeds provides safe spaces and transformative learning environments that enable adolescents and young adults to successfully transition into adulthood. With a unique 'SPECS' for raising young people, Young Breeds ministers to the needs of young people, investing in their Spiritual, Physical, Emotional, Cognitive and Social development of young people. Discover more at www.youngbreeds.org

Dr. Abraham's extraordinary teaching capabilities and exceptional communication skills have translated into enriched learning experiences in his subject discipline as a seasoned university lecturer, establishing a robust teaching and research reputation.

As an advocate for change, he has conceptualised and spearheaded various development initiatives, successfully inspiring and mobilising transformational advocacy work, educational programs, and community development projects.

His expertise is frequently sought after for keynote addresses, public lectures, workshops, and knowledge-sharing sessions across diverse media platforms, both in-person and virtually. Non-profit organisations, educational districts, corporations, schools, small and medium-sized enterprises (SMEs), and faith-based institutions have turned to him to address issues related to the growth of young people, and holistic skills development.

Dr. Abraham's educational programs and youth development interventions have positively impacted over 20,000 young individuals since 2011. His extensive media presence on radio and TV, with hundreds of keynotes and public lectures delivered, books, training programs, online courses, podcasts, and scientific articles have profoundly touched the hearts and minds of thousands across Africa, North America, Asia, and Europe. Described consistently as transformational, inspirational, persuasive, knowledgeable, passionate, and empathetic, Dr. Abraham has left an indelible mark on individuals worldwide.

Driven by a vision of a world where human minds are well-moulded to achieve personal and corporate goals, Dr. Abraham Owoseni serves as the Lead Trainer of MindMould, a training, publishing, and human development agency. MindMould equips individuals and institutions with the mental resources necessary to multiply productivity and profitability by offering unique learning solutions, leadership training services, and upscaling leadership competencies, thereby empowering corporations and businesses to enhance their impact and achieve greater success.

Additionally, Dr. Abraham serves as the Dean of the Life Harmony Mentorship School, an edtech institution where he mentors young adults in gaining clarity of purpose and direction in their careers, relationships, and lifestyle to achieve all-round success and lead wholesome lives.

With a PhD focusing on educational infrastructure and learning environments, Dr. Abraham Owoseni's academic excellence, reinforced by multiple certifications in areas like education, productivity, life coaching, digital communication, social innovation, neuro-cognitive consonance, lean Six Sigma, leadership, pedagogy, and a first-class degree in architecture has earned him over 18 prestigious awards and academic recognitions.

Dr. Abraham Owoseni is not only a dedicated leader but also a devoted family man; he is a life partner to his wife Sarah, an esteemed educator and family life practitioner. They are the proud parents of Isaac and Daniel, united in their mission to fulfill God's purpose with global impact.

Dr. Abraham continues to advance Sustainable Development Goals 4 (Quality Education), 8 (Decent Work and Economic Growth), and 11 (Sustainable Cities and Communities) through his unwavering commitment. For further details on Dr. Abraham Owoseni and his impactful work, please visit www.abrahamowoseni.com

Connect with Dr. Abraham Owoseni:

Email:	ab@abrahamowoseni.com
Instagram:	@abrahamowoseni
LinkedIn:	@abrahamowoseni
Facebook:	@LifeSkillsExpert
Twitter:	@AbrahamOwoseni
YouTube:	@AbrahamOwoseni

Final Notes

What's next? Take a moment to reflect on your experience from this resource, what are your final thoughts? Make a note of them. What resonated with you the most?

Most Pressing Action Points

What immediate steps would you take in your journey of putting your learning to work